RESCUED

A woman's guide to surviving
and thriving after sexual betrayal

by SHELLEY S. MARTINKUS

Thank you for allowing me a safe place to work toward being fully known.
And in that fully known, thanks for loving and accepting all of me.

TABLE OF CONTENTS

HOW TO USE THIS WORKBOOK

I highly recommend that you use this workbook within a group setting. There are many options for groups through local churches or over the phone. Refer to appendix A on page 137 for the set-up and framework of the group. It always works best to have a point person that is facilitating the group and keeping the group on track. I have found that ninety-minute group sessions every other week work well. And close to five participants seems to be the sweet spot, but go with what you've got.

If you are working through this material on your own, consider reaching out to find someone else with a similar story to journey with you through these pages. I believe you will get so much more from doing this in community.

Use the first couple of sessions to share your story. More details found in appendix A.

I've tried to organize the chapters in a natural order but keep in mind; this process is definitely not linear. So feel free to skip around a bit depending on the needs of the group as the weeks go by. I'd recommend saving the last three to four chapters for the very end.

Also, I've found it's important to switch back and forth between curriculum and checking-in. The check-in's are just as important if not more important than the curriculum. So make sure that if you spend a session discussing curriculum, the next session should be reserved for a check-in. The check-in format is found on page 139-140.

Appendix E, starting on page 157 contains twenty session notes. You can organize your questions and thoughts before your support group meeting and after your session; fill out The One Thing, which is explained on page 137-138.

And last, know that I'd love to hear from you and help you get plugged into a group. Please feel free to email me at Shelley@rlforwomen.com.

Grateful,

Shelley

INTRODUCTION

It was never my intention to write a workbook for wives as they try to heal after sexual betrayal has rocked their world. Little did I know, but the seeds of this workbook started to take root more than five years ago when I started my first support group through Redemptive Living for Women. I had very little prepared as far as a framework for the group. We shared our stories, decided on and discussed our goals, and proceeded to meet every other week to bring our ugly into the light. Although I served as the facilitator for the group, over time, I realized I needed this kind of support in my life, too. It's as if I was floundering out at sea – only my life preserver and me. But what I needed to do was find a boat and climb aboard. I needed a safe place where I could be real. A place were I could be transparent and vulnerable and work through my suitcase of hidden darkness. The lifeboat was right under my nose. So after our one-year anniversary, I asked the gals if I could step down as the facilitator and instead we could take turns co-leading. God had finally given me my Go-To Girls. And this was a huge part of my rescue. It was in this little group that I started to learn how to be fully known and also how to fully know another.

It was in part because of my Go-To Girls that I finally mustered the courage to quit the job that I had held close to my heart for twelve years. I knew God wanted me to encourage and equip women and I just didn't have the bandwidth to do this all the while working part-time outside the home. Shortly after my resignation, I started four more groups with two of those being over the phone. My days were filled with caring for two little boys, facilitating these groups and pouring myself into books to learn as much as I could. I would take what I was learning back to the groups. This was yet another step towards preparing this workbook for wives.

About six months into leading these groups, Jason and I received the surprise of our lives when we found out we were pregnant with our third son. Shortly after his birth, all my groups (except my Go-To Girls) came to a close and I became confused and disillusioned with God's plan. I simply didn't see a third baby being a part of the reason I resigned from my career some thirteen months prior. I thought God wanted me to help wives, not rear another precious baby boy.

When Norman, our third son, was about 13 months old, I hit rock bottom. I didn't realize it but I had been suffering from post-partum depression. It was a very scary time for me. I was filled with fear. As Jason and I started to pick up the pieces, I knew that part of my self-care plan needed to be my return to work. Even if very part-time,

I needed an outlet. I went back to my Go-To Girls to get their input. Should I try to facilitate groups? Or should I return to the world of Physical Therapy? I listened to their input. And it became clear that opening myself up to facilitating groups was the best choice. Not only that, but I needed to go all in. Go all in or go home.

It was God and only God that brought six groups comprised of 31 women into my life shortly after. Because I was all in, I decided I needed to prepare material for these groups. I used some of my material from the groups prior and started crafting new material for needs as they came up. The material started to take a life of its own and before I knew it, I had a workbook!

Workbook is a very appropriate name for what you are holding. It will most certainly be hard work to read through these pages and answer the questions. I know that there are some things I'm sharing within these pages that 12, 24, even 36 months in, I wouldn't have wanted to hear. You might want to throw the book across the room. You might feel defensive. If you do, know that chances are, I'm hitting on a sensitive area. It's okay. We all have these areas in our hearts that need healing. Hopefully you are working through this workbook with a group. If so, I encourage you to loop back to them as questions and feelings surface.

Last, I want you to know, if you are holding this workbook, you are a woman worth being rescued. Right now, you might feel like you are just keeping your head above water. Or it might be that right at this moment, you feel like you are drowning. I know this because I was there. I was treading water before a life preserver was thrown my way. And it wasn't until I found real support from my Go-To Girls that I made it to the boat and I climbed aboard.

So please hear me say: there is hope for you. There is a boat waiting for you. The timeline is different for everyone but at some point, you will climb aboard the boat and take a deep breath.

It's my hope that this workbook will serve as a conduit for getting you out of the tumultuous sea and into the boat. The journey never ends. But I can tell you that the sea calms down. You will find the peace and joy you are looking for. It IS possible. So keep moving forward.

CHAPTER ONE

Understanding Sexual Integrity Issues and Sexual Addiction

Before you start to dig into yourself through the pages of this book, I think it's important that you have a solid foundation in understanding both sexual integrity issues as well as sexual addiction. After all, that's what has brought us all together.

THE DIFFERENCE BETWEEN A SEXUAL INTEGRITY ISSUE AND A SEXUAL ADDICTION

Oftentimes, when trying to explain the concept of a sexual addiction, a debate ensues over the parameters and the explicit definition of an addiction of this nature. Keep in mind that in the Diagnostic and Statistical Manual of Disorders, which is the standard created and used by the medical community for defining mental health issues, a sexual addiction is not considered a bona fide disorder. It has been hotly debated and in the end, the most current revisions of the manual ruled out sex addiction. While sex addiction didn't meet all the criteria, there are three key components of "addiction" that we can apply from the medical community's definitions: 1) mood altering, 2) impairs functioning, and 3) difficulty stopping even when desiring to.

On the other hand, a sexual integrity issue, I propose, is more of an umbrella term used to describe someone that may (or may not) have an addiction per se but has breached their marriage covenant by acting out sexually in some form or fashion, whether once or a sundry of times, mentally, emotionally and/or physically.

Debating with your husband as to whether or not he has a sexual addiction may not be worth your breath. Whether it is an addiction or an integrity issue, it hurts just the same. For this reason, I use the terms interchangeably throughout this material. Try not to let this be a distraction. All of the concepts apply to a wife healing from the damage caused by a husband with either a sexual addiction or a sexual integrity issue.

In addition, I use the word "wife" consistently but know that whether you are married, divorced, engaged or dating; whether your marriage ends or is restored; every woman impacted by sexual betrayal is worthy of healing. Each of you is welcome here. Don't forget your comfy pants, grab something warm to drink and let's dig in together!

Now that you have an understanding of the aforementioned terms, it's also important to have a grasp of the addictive cycle since it explains some of the thoughts and feelings behind your husband's actions.

As you look at the addictive cycle (see figure 1.1)[1] , it's important to remember that a trigger could potentially be anything. However, we can boil it down to three key things, **shame**, (known as the three I's, which we will discuss in greater detail in chapter nine), **a negative emotion**, or even the **desire to reward oneself**.

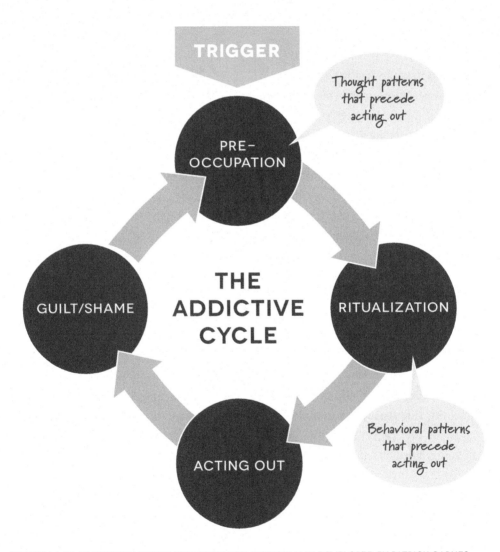

FIGURE 1.1 AN ADAPTATION OF THE ADDICTIVE CYCLE ORIGINALLY DEVELOPED BY PATRICK CARNES.

For now, know that the "male version" of the three I's are **Insignificance** (Do I matter?), **Incompetence** (Do I have what it takes?) and **Impotence** (Do I have power or control?). (There is a female version, too which I will also discuss in chapter nine). When one of these three I's is activated, your husband will then start to look for ways to medicate so that he doesn't have to feel these strong emotions. Keep in mind that early in recovery he may not even be able to identify that this is what is going on inside of him.

In order to explain the addictive cycle, let's use an example. There was once a man (that shall remain nameless) working for a large corporation who hated his job. He didn't feel that he was well suited for his line of work. He felt very incompetent at what he did. One particular day his boss got onto him because of his performance. He was **triggered** (but didn't have the insight to be aware of this). He felt so incompetent that all he could think about was getting home and getting his fix. It was almost as if he was in a trance and nothing would stop him (**preoccupation**). He left his office early without even considering the consequences. He arrived at home and knew his wife wouldn't be home for a couple of hours. He grabbed cold pizza out of the fridge and sat down on the couch. He opened up his computer and decided to check stock quotes, sports highlights and YouTube. He clicked on these things almost every time before looking at porn (**ritualization**). Then he started to look at pornography. He viewed it for about fifteen minutes before quickly shutting his computer. He couldn't believe that he did it again. If his wife knew, she would leave him, he was sure of it. He felt so **guilty** for doing it. Again. He told himself he was worthless and not deserving of his wife's love. He was **ashamed** of himself.

While oversimplified, I hope this example scenario gives you an idea of how acting out works. Now let's look at the acting out continuum.

THE "ACTING OUT" CONTINUUM

Acting out looks completely different for each person. Let's think of this using a continuum (see figure 1.2). On the left end is sexual lust - sinful thought patterns of sexual fantasy. These things are contained in the mind, not acted out in real life. As you move to the right on the continuum, the sinful activities move from thought life to real, lived life. The level of depravity, gravity of consequence as well as compulsivity all increase as well. This is not to say that the sin is "worse" as you move to the right, but it is to say that the sin is different, with different consequences.

One would assume that as you move from left to right on the continuum, the level of pain the wife feels also increases. But this is actually very inaccurate. Yes, the level of consequences for both the wife and her husband increase when moving from left to right on the continuum (for example, exposure to STD's), but not necessarily the pain. We can't judge someone else's pain nor do we know the sum of their life experiences prior to disclosure or discovery. I state this in order to validate your pain. It's not "just masturbation" or "just pornography". This behavior can, in all possibilities, be just as damaging as a one-night stand or anything else. There are simply too many variables that go into each of our stories. My pain is my pain and your pain is your pain.

CONTINUUM OF SEXUALLY ACTING OUT

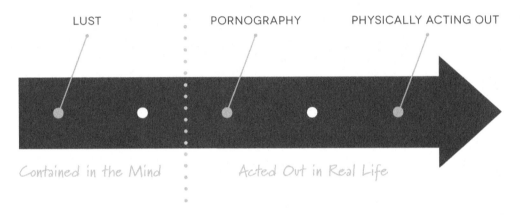

FIGURE 1.2 CONSEQUENCES INCREASE WHEN MOVING FROM LEFT TO RIGHT BUT NOT NECESSARILY THE WIFE'S PAIN.

IT'S SO PERSONAL

Being married to a man with a sexual integrity issue and/or a sexual addiction, I believe is the most painful of addictions out there. It feels ever so personal for a wife, and rightfully so. When a spouse is addicted to alcohol or drugs, their partner realizes that they are choosing these substances over them and they are choosing these substances over becoming healthier. I'm not trying to lessen the damage and hurt that such choices make in a relationship. I'm simply proposing that choosing alcohol over a spouse doesn't feel as personal as **when a husband chooses other women over his own wife**. Very quickly, the comparison begins between you and the other woman. Whether it's porn, lust, affairs, or prostitutes, the comparison begins. And you begin to ask yourself: Why? What is so wrong with me? Why would he choose her over myself?

(It's important to note that some men don't act out with other women but instead act out with men, animals, inanimate objects, or within their minds. All of these modes of acting out are hurtful. Throughout this workbook, I refer to "other women" because that is often the case but depending on your situation, feel free to substitute the language that fits your story.)

QUESTION #1: When you realized your husband had a sexual integrity issue, did you compare yourself to the women he was using? Did you wonder why your husband was choosing his sexual addiction over you? If your husband disclosed that he was acting out with other men, how did this affect you?

As you start to sit with the fact that your husband chose another woman over you, it's natural to think that you did something wrong. That in some way, this was your fault. If you were more attractive, sexier, skinnier, had larger breasts or smaller breasts, had more curves, had brown hair, had blonde hair (really, you could plug literally anything in here) then this wouldn't have happened. But the reality is: **It's not your fault.** The truth of the matter is, you did not choose nor force your husband to look for sexual pleasure outside of your relationship. Sure, there are certain personality characteristics that you brought into your relationship that may have pushed his buttons in an unhealthy way, but that is no excuse for a husband's choices. **We are all responsible for our own actions, but not for each other's actions.**

QUESTION #2: Do you believe in your heart AND in your mind that your husband's sexual integrity issues are NOT your fault? Why or why not? (Note that sometimes what you know in your mind and what your heart feels are two distinct things.)

With any coping mechanism a person uses, it is important to figure out what is driving the behavior. Because a sexual integrity issue is in its simplest sense a coping mechanism, it's imperative that your husband is able to identify the very thing at the core of his onion that drove him into this destructive and damaging behavior.

Almost all the time, at the core of the onion for men struggling with these sorts of behaviors is a core belief that they are **unwanted** and **unloved**.[2] Keep in mind that these holes in your husband's heart started growing in childhood, well before he met you. Deep down your husband feels unloved, unwanted, and even abandoned. In fact, the sense of abandonment - some believe - is seen as the most influential contributor to a sexual addiction.[3] This "sense of abandonment" could present itself explicitly (a caregiver leaving the family), implicitly (a caregiver dying during childhood) or even in the form of a threat (a caregiver threatening to leave). With this in mind, it might be that at first glance, your husband says he doesn't believe he was abandoned. His mom was there. But as the hard work of peeling back the layers ensues, typically there is a sense of abandonment present. At the core of abandonment is this: "you don't *want* me."

Patrick Carnes says that these core beliefs (think of these core beliefs as the lens we view the world through, in other words, it influences our choices) build upon one another until ultimately, the addict believes that his most important need is sex.[4] (You may be saying, *"Hold up...I'm starting to take this personal. I loved him I accepted him. What did I do wrong?"* Remember: This isn't about how much love you've given but rather the core beliefs from childhood that have influenced your husband's choices.)

If you feel especially responsible for your husband's behavior – it might be worth looking back at **your** family of origin. Did you put others needs before yours? Was the role you played in your family that of the caretaker? If so, then it makes sense that you'd feel especially responsible for not meeting every need of your husband. So here is the truth: you can't meet your husband's every need. It's simply impossible. Just like he can't meet every one of your needs. In addition, remember, just because your husband's needs were not met (whether perceived or in reality) doesn't give him the right to expend his sexual energy elsewhere.

I hope you are tracking with me because this next sentence is important: it's through this addiction or integrity issue that your husband was able to manufacture feeling wanted, loved and accepted. Think about it: will your husband get rejected when he looks at porn? Will he get rejected when he goes to a strip club? Will he get rejected when he chooses to masturbate? The answer is no. This in turn causes a **false intimacy** to develop. This isn't true intimacy between a husband and a wife; this is fabricated self-preserving intimacy between your man and whatever sexual fantasy or act he so chooses. (I will discuss this in greater detail in chapter twelve.) Thus, a husband with a sexual integrity issue typically isn't very connected to himself or the people close to him. He never learned how to be emotionally intimate with others.

It's common for me to hear a wife say she "never hears her husband share his feelings". The reason being: a man with an integrity issue or addiction doesn't know how to connect with himself or with others. **Remember – true intimacy requires being fully known and fully knowing (another).**

THE SEXUAL INTEGRITY ISSUE IS PERVASIVE

If you think this destructive behavior has only affected your sexual relationship with your husband, think again. When a man is devoting any amount of time to any part of the continuum mentioned above, it affects multiple areas of the couple's life.

I think two of the best words to describe a man with a sexual integrity issue are: detached and selfish. I can speak first hand to this. During our first couple of years of marriage, I felt like I was responsible for everything: paying the bills, oil changes, grocery shopping, home maintenance; all the while we both worked full-time outside the home. In addition, I remember wanting so badly to connect with Jason in some way. About three years into our marriage, I still remember chasing him through our house trying to engage in an argument with him. He eventually locked himself in a bathroom and chose not to come out.

THE SEXUAL INTEGRITY ISSUE IS A SECRET

A hallmark of this addiction/integrity issue is the fact that it is done when nobody is watching. It's something that most men say they'd never share and instead believe they will take it with them to their graves. If and when a wife finds out about her husband's secrets, it's extremely difficult for her to reach out for help. This in turn perpetuates the problem. Know that you are not alone when you are walking in these shoes. For example, one recent study found that sixty-three percent of those men surveyed admitted to "looking at pornography at least one time *while at work* in the last three months" (emphasis mine).[5] If that doesn't surprise you then how about this: every second, 30,000 people view porn and there are sixty-eight million porn searches *per day*.[6] And last, roughly twelve billion dollars is spent on the sex industry per year in the United States alone (fifty-seven billion world-wide).[7] Indeed, if you are a wife that has been impacted by sexual betrayal, you most definitely are not alone.

Remember, what your husband has chosen to engage in isn't about you. It was *his* choice. It isn't *your* fault. With that being said, it's still painfully personal and hurtful. Whether your husband has engaged in activities towards the left of the continuum or towards the right, I want to validate that it is all very painful.

CHAPTER TWO

The Difference between Trauma, Codependency and a Co-Addict

For many years, the spouse of an addict has been labeled as a co-addict or codependent person. However, in recent years, there has been more and more talk of the spouse being one that is traumatized. In *Your Sexually Addicted Spouse*, authors Barbara Steffens and Marsha Means suggest that this label (co-addict/codependent) is inaccurate and treatment for the spouse falls short when using this paradigm alone.[8] In fact, from Steffens research, she has found that seventy percent of the women she researched "met the symptomatic criteria for PTSD (Post Traumatic Stress Disorder) in response to the disclosure of sexual addiction".[9]

I think it's important that you understand all of these concepts. Some women may exhibit codependency (or co-addiction) in their relationship with their husband and some may not. By having a clear understanding of these concepts, you can become more insightful throughout your journey. If you start to see any warning signs of co-addiction or codependency, you can do the necessary work to move forward past these labels. So let's start with discussing these labels.

CODEPENDENCY

If you've read Melody Beattie's *Codependent No More*, you will come across multiple definitions for a codependent. Beattie even says, "I'm not trying to confuse you. Codependency has a fuzzy definition because it is a gray, fuzzy condition. It is complex, theoretical and difficult to define in one or two sentences."[10] From the research I've done I couldn't agree more. It seems there isn't one solid definition that everyone uses but rather many definitions with commonalities.

With that being said, here is a description of a codependent: typically a codependent is in a relationship with a needy, dependent and oftentimes addicted person. Thus, a codependent can be thought of as fulfilling a helper type role within the relationship. The codependent's behavior and the addict's behavior synergistically cause more and more unhealthy patterns and take both partners further from health and healing. The codependent person ends up enabling the addict. Think of enablement as "covering up for the addict, protecting him or her from consequences, and keeping silent about personal concerns".[11] The unhealthy patterns, while damaging and ineffective relationally, provide a familiarity and a false sense of security that are easier to maintain than to change.

To further complicate things; there can be silent rules within the relationship that promote both the codependent's behavior as well as the addict's behavior.
For example:
- "We don't discuss our problems, we just hope they'll go away"
- "We don't talk about feelings or vulnerabilities"
- "We're fine just the way we are"

Overall, an environment develops that does not promote authenticity or personal growth.[12]

QUESTION #1: Do you think this description of a codependent describes you? Or is this different than what you thought of when you heard the word codependent?

CO-ADDICTION

You may be wondering about the term co-addict. And it's quite interesting how this term came about. Understand first that in the 12-step program of Alcoholics Anonymous (AA), any spouse of the addict was labeled as a codependent. Patrick Carnes and other early pioneers in the sex addiction field came onto the scene and realized that a sex-addict could fit into the AA addiction recovery model. But these early researchers took it one step further. They felt that the partners of a sex-addict *were addicted to the addict* and thus coined the term co-addict. Just to be clear, the term co-addict *only* applies to partners in relationship with a sexual addict, not any other type of addiction.[13] A simple definition of a co-addict is as follows: "a family member that becomes so involved in (another's) addiction that they participate in the illness."[14]

Just as an addict has a set of core beliefs, as mentioned in chapter one, that influence how he sees the world and the choices he makes, Carnes suggests that a co-addict also has a set of core beliefs. These core beliefs are as follows: 1) "I am basically a bad and unworthy person." 2) "No one would love me as I am." 3) "My needs are never going to be met if I have to depend on others." And these core beliefs culminate with the final belief: 4) "Sex is the most important sign of love."[15]

It might be that you relate to some of the characteristics of a co-addict, or you might not. For myself, I really relate to core belief three from above. I truly felt like my needs were never going to be met by anyone but myself. I entered into my relationship with Jason with this core belief already intact. And when Jason shared his ugly truth with me, it further confirmed that I, Shelley, was the only person I could rely on.

QUESTION #2: What about for you, can you relate to any of the characteristics of a co-addict?

With that being said, please hear me say, for myself and for many women, being labeled a co-addict bears a burden that we can't justifiably own. It assumes that you hold as much responsibility for your husband's actions as your husband does. In the wake of discovering the ugly truth about your husband, when you feel the least safe and the least secure because of the depth of the betrayal, to be told that you somehow share responsibility or that you have an addiction to your husband is almost too much to bear. I have heard countless stories from women who go to see a well-meaning counselor or pastor who, instead of validating their pain and heartbreak, turn to the wife and ask, "So what was your responsibility in this mess?" In fact, I share this story as well. The first counselor Jason and I saw said these exact words, which I will never forget. I don't even remember how I responded but I do remember crying uncontrollably and as soon as we left this counselor's office, I told Jason I would never see said counselor again.

I will say this until I am blue in the face – you are not *responsible* for your husband's poor choices. You did not force your husband to do the things he did that betrayed you.

TRAUMA

In contrast to the co-addiction and codependency models, the trauma model is used to describe a spouse that is *reacting* to the fact that their world and their marriage isn't what they thought it was. The spouse is searching for safety and security. They yearn to be heard. They desire for their husband to empathize with them and understand their pain. Ignoring this trauma is a recipe for disaster. It will somehow, someway, seep its way out if it isn't discussed and processed. Steffens and Means report that ninety percent of illnesses are caused by stress and certainly, the trauma caused by a sexual integrity issue is no exception.[16]

STAYING AFLOAT

In the early stages of the healing process, I don't think it is helpful to spend a lot of time getting caught up in the co-addict and codependency labels. For any wife that goes through the chain of events that leads to finding out that her husband doesn't only have eyes for her but also has eyes for others, whether acted out in his heart or acted out in real life, there will be a certain amount of trauma that this wife sustains. If this trauma isn't dealt with it could turn into a more serious form of trauma, which is post-traumatic stress disorder.

Sure, there will be wives that exhibit codependent and co-addict characteristics. For some wives, you'll need to get the help of a counselor and work through how you can be healthier in your relationships both with your spouse as well as with others. The time frame for working through these issues is different for each wife. Also, remember that chances are each of us exhibits hints of these behaviors in any given relationship.

You might want to consider reading *Your Sexually Addicted Spouse* by Barbara Steffens and Marsha Means and *Out of the Shadows* by Patrick Carnes for a more in depth discussion of these concepts. I will warn you that both books are triggering and early on in my recovery, I would not have been able to read them.

And last, if you feel you are experiencing a significant amount of stress from the trauma of sexual betrayal, it's imperative to find a qualified counselor to help you navigate through this piece of the process. You are not alone in what you are feeling and there is help for you.

CHAPTER THREE

Loving Yourself Well — Se

Next, look at th
ities have y
Circle th
additi
a f

WHAT IS SELF CARE?

Self Care is an important component of your journey. In fact, practicing heal...
care is a non-negotiable when you are barely keeping your head above water.

Think of self-care as the many things you can do *to love yourself well* which in turn
promotes healthiness to the fullest. There are many strategies you can use to work on
loving yourself well and that is what this chapter is going to focus on.

EMPTY ME/FILL ME UP

One of these strategies to help with self-care is identifying activities and people in
your life that empty you, and activities and people in your life that fill you up. Use the
table below to start to think through what fills you up and what depletes your energy.
This will look different for every person. Keep in mind that just because something or
someone drains you, doesn't mean it is a bad thing or should be avoided. Rather, the
goal is to make sure there is balance in your life between the activities that empty you
and fill you up, not necessarily altogether avoiding certain activities or people.

PEOPLE/ACTIVITIES THAT **FILL ME UP**	PEOPLE/ACTIVITIES THAT **EMPTY ME**

activities you listed in the "fill me up" column. Which of these activ-

done in the last twenty-four hours? What about in the last three days?

m. Your goal should be to do at least one or two of these activities **daily**. In

on, during the more stressful times of this process, for instance, when you hear

ull disclosure from your husband, plan out a couple of these activities after your

session that will help recharge you and fill you up. Be intentional to take time for yourself. If you are having trouble thinking of some activities to help refill your tank, refer to appendix B on page 147 for healthy self-care strategies.

SELF-INTIMACY

Another concept that helps with self-care is to know yourself, listen to yourself and respect yourself. This is called self-intimacy. Laurel Mellin states that when you are faced with a stressful situation, **if you know yourself well, you can securely attach to yourself.** On the other hand, if you aren't able to soothe and comfort yourself, you will look outside yourself for comfort (this is called an external solution). She says by completing the following sentence, you know what your external solutions might be: "I get my safety (love, nurturing, security) from _____."[17]

Another word for an external solution is a coping mechanism. List your current coping mechanisms (healthy and unhealthy) as well as past coping mechanisms that you use when you are stressed.

	MY **HEALTHY** COPING MECHANISMS	MY **UNHEALTHY** COPING MECHANISMS
CURRENT		
PAST		

It's important for you to consider the cost of your unhealthy and destructive behaviors. In the margin, jot down what your unhealthy coping mechanism is costing you. For example, an unhealthy coping mechanism for myself is negative self-talk. When I listen and believe the negative self-talk in my head, it's costing me in several ways. It's costing me emotional stability, peace and freedom, to name a few.

As you begin to listen to yourself and meet your own needs in a healthy way, your propensity for coping in destructive and unhealthy ways decreases.

Below is an easy way for you to begin working towards this end. It was my girlfriend Jill that brought this to our group one evening. She had been working with a counselor and the counselor was encouraging Jill to hone in on how she feels rather than thinking about everyone else's preferences first. (As a side note, Jill self-admittedly struggled with how she told herself she *ought* to feel versus identifying how she actually felt. Can any of you relate to Jill's struggle?) The four questions were revolutionary for our little group!

The Four Questions:
1.   **What do I think?**
2.   **What do I want?**
3.   **What do I need?**
4.   **What do I feel?**

Utilizing these **Four Questions** can help you on multiple fronts. First, know that simply identifying your needs/wants/feelings, etc. allows yourself clarity, freedom and self-empowerment – even if you don't act on them right away. There is something so freeing about identifying where you are at and allowing yourself to rest there. Second, through using these **Four Questions**, you can better understand yourself, thus developing self-intimacy. And last, this tool is an excellent resource to use when faced with a dilemma or stressor.

Let me give you an example from my life. This past summer, Jason and I went with extended family to Red River, NM. Jason had expressed on the first day that he wanted to go on a long hike to the top of Mt. Wheeler. I told him that sounded like fun and we should do it. But as the day of the hike approached, I started to feel like it wouldn't be do-able. So, the night before, as we were continuing to make our plans for the early morning hike, Jason could tell that I wasn't on board. I hadn't even realized how stressed I was about the hike. After a couple of conversations, I realized that I was afraid to express to him how I really felt. The truth was, I didn't **think** the hike was a good idea. I **felt** overwhelmed with the task of waking up early and making sure our three boys would be well taken care of by extended family. I **wanted** instead for the day to be relaxing. I **needed** a pass on the hike. But I was so afraid of disappointing Jason, that I wasn't being true to myself and expressing my needs. Once I was able to release the fact that I may disappoint Jason (because I can't control him or his emotions), I was able to express the above to him. Although he was disappointed, he also understood. We agreed to scrap the hike and plan better next go around.

Now it's your turn to practice. Think of a couple of times over the last week where you might have made a choice that didn't quite match how you were feeling inside. Use the table below to work through the situations.

	SITUATION #1	SITUATION #2
EXPLAIN THE SITUATION		
WHAT DO I THINK?		
WHAT DO I WANT?		
WHAT DO I NEED?		
WHAT DO I FEEL?		
OUTCOME		

It's important to keep in mind that as you answer these four questions, you aren't answering for what your husband (boyfriend, ex-husband) thinks/wants/needs/feels or for what your best friend thinks/wants/needs/feels. Basically, you aren't thinking about anyone else but yourself as you answer these questions. You are being completely honest with yourself about what you think/want/need/feel. *You are finding your voice.*

Something that has proved helpful to me is to check-in on these things with myself throughout the day. Commit to asking yourself the think/want/need/feel questions at least three times a day, whether you are in a stressed state or not.

OTHER SELF CARE STRATEGIES

See below for strategies that are important for you to use and work through in order for you to take care of yourself well.

SELF-SOOTHING TECHNIQUES

When you are stressed, it's important that you have a couple of tricks up your sleeve that really work for you - to not only ground yourself but also love on yourself. You can certainly use the lists above (activities that fill you up and healthy coping mechanisms) as a starting point. Table 3.1 on page 22 lists some other suggestions to incorporate into your life.

UNDERSTANDING AND IMPLEMENTING DETACHMENT

Another strategy that you can use during the early stages of recovery is known as **detachment**. Think of detachment as an intentional "buffer" between you and your spouse. To be clear, detachment isn't to be used as a way of punishing your spouse but rather to create safety and peace within yourself.[18] Without realizing it, this is something I did early on with Jason. It's almost as if I took a large step back from our relationship and replaced my glasses of denial with my glasses of truth. I started to see myself, Jason and our marriage for what it really was; lies, manipulation and false intimacy. I started to take all the hurts and situations that I had stuffed under the rug and place them on the coffee table. I looked at them for what they truly were. I slowly came to terms with the fact that my marriage may not survive. Furthermore, I realized that I didn't even know that I wanted to stay married to Jason, even if he were to make the hard changes. I expressed this to him - not in the posture of condemnation or self-righteousness but rather in a detached, "letting go of" sort of way.

COGNITIVE/EMOTIONAL SELF-CARE

- When in the depths of despair, it's beneficial to remind yourself that "this, too, will pass". This isn't a way of invalidating pain but rather when you are feeling intense pain, you can remind yourself that after you get it out, you will feel some relief.

- Oftentimes early in the process, you replay the hurts you are dealing with over and over again like a rotisserie grill in your mind. There are times when it is okay to give yourself permission to stop the thoughts. This is called a Brain Stop. Saying out loud "Stop, I'm not going to think about this right now" can help you stop the spinning.

- Reading books a little more on the light and funny side as well as not triggering. Here are a few books I've read recently that fit the bill: *The Antelope In The Living Room, Sparkly Green Earrings, A Little Salty to Cut the Sweet.*

- Reading books about sexual integrity issues. For instance, I found *When Good Men are Tempted* by Bill Perkins to be an easier book to digest. I still find that books on this subject can be triggering for me, so use caution here.

PHYSICAL SELF-CARE

- Exercise – try to move daily. Find something that will help you connect to your body all the while helping you feel better.

- Sunlight – Vitamin D is thought to help decrease depression and anxiety.

- Pampering yourself – A massage, pedi/mani, and/or a bubble bath to name a few.

SPIRITUAL SELF-CARE

- Socializing with girlfriends – it may be that you have to force yourself to get out and meet with the people you love. It's okay for a period of time to be choosy about those you meet up with, but make it a point to get together with some of your favorite people and enjoy time together.

- Taking time to listen to music that speaks to your soul. This was a highly effective tool for me during the first couple of years of our recovery.

- Dwelling on the book of Psalms. Make it a point to read one chapter a day.

- Journaling your thoughts and prayers to God

- Breath Prayer – come up with a small prayer that you can say over and over again under your breath. This should be a set of words that speaks deeply to your soul. For instance, something I remind myself of is: *"Shelley, I am fearfully and wonderfully made. I am worth it. I have what it takes."* What is a breath prayer that you can repeat to yourself? Write it in the margin.

TABLE 3.1 SELF-SOOTHING STRATEGIES

Detachment can be a hard concept to fully grasp. I believe it is also difficult to know if your detachment is healthy. Here is a word picture that might help as you make sense of what detachment can look like:

- **Spectator in the Stands** – When you are practicing detachment in a healthy way, you choose to not be on the defense or the offense (toward your husband). Instead, you take a seat in the stands and eat some popcorn. You continue to watch and wait. But you aren't getting on the field and engaging in the game.[19]

Another way to look at detachment is on a continuum. On the left side is a crazy, chaos and co-dependent connection with our husband. On the right is denial and apathy. In the middle is where you are healthy and detached. You allow both grace and truth. As you think about this continuum, refer to Table 3.2 for what detachment is and what detachment is not.

HEALTHY DETACHMENT IS...

- Safety.
- Loving myself.
- Feet firmly planted and looking at the big picture.
- Giving myself permission to enjoy his company when I feel safe.
- Empowering.
- An active (never ending) and intentional process.
- Ultimately trusting God.
- Possibly a physical separation.
- Taking a step back.
- Recognizing and believing: "I can't fix him."
- Necessary.
- Finding your voice.
- Centered and Grounded.
- Strong.
- Responding (versus reacting).

HEALTHY DETACHMENT IS NOT...

- Control.
- Fight or Flight.
- Scanning the environment for attractive women that your husband might take a second look at.
- Codependency.
- Denial.
- Abandonment.
- Reacting (versus responding).
- Apathy.
- Ignoring or being rude.
- Cold.
- Being stepped on.
- Validating the dysfunction.

TABLE 3.2 DETACHMENT IS/DETACHMENT IS NOT

With that in mind, following are three elements core to this concept of detachment:

- **First, I recognize my powerlessness to change my husband.** You simply can't change your husband. Only he can choose into making those changes, with God's help. And sometimes the greatest gift you can give him is to step back and allow him to make the changes and the mistakes along the way.

- **Second, I will choose to embrace my power to create safety for myself.** This is all about using your voice and clinging to empowerment. Ask yourself: *"what do I need?"* and *"what can I do today to take care of myself?"*

- **Third, I commit to watching and waiting and giving God the space to cultivate that change in my marriage that I so desire.** You choose to trust in God. To release your husband and your marriage to him. I will discuss this more in chapter twelve on rebuilding trust.

QUESTION #1: What does detachment look like for you during this process? Write down what you can do to protect yourself emotionally and create safety for yourself all the while giving God the opportunity to do a good work in your husband.

PERMISSION TO TAKE A BREAK

Taking a break can be seen from two different angles. The first angle is to simply put a stop to any and all outside commitments. No matter the season you find yourself in, whether it's retirement, working parent, stay-at-home mom, student or working professional; I bet your life is busy. Thus, it's important to unplug. Look at your commitments and decide what you can release for a period of time. In addition, give yourself permission to say "no" to opportunities that might come your way in the near future. During this delicate period of time, chances are extra commitments would increase your stress level.

QUESTION #2: What commitments in your life right now do you feel you need to unplug from? Will it be hard for you to set a different boundary with a group or person and let them know that you need to take a step back? If so, why?

Below are a couple of suggestions as you give yourself permission to take a break:

- Remember, you don't owe people an explanation. It's not necessary to go into detail about the ins and outs of why you have come to this decision. You can simply say that you are under a lot of stress and it's important that you step back from some commitments for a season.

- Be forewarned, not everyone will respond well to your commitment to prioritizing yourself and your needs before theirs. It can feel like another hurt, especially when your heart already feels vulnerable. Remind yourself that you are doing what is best for *you* and what is best for *your family* in order to get to the other side.

The second angle on giving yourself permission to take a break is specifically in regards to your healing process. Early on in our recovery, our counselor encouraged Jason and I to take time outs from the heavy processing. We would intentionally agree on an evening where we weren't going to talk about our recovery and instead go do something special together. This was especially difficult for me because I felt like I was faking it, but it proved to be a helpful strategy for us to allow ourselves a period of time where we were off-line. We were able to put our differences and hurts aside for a period of a couple of hours all the while knowing we'd pick up where we left off after the date.

QUESTION #3: What do you think about this concept of taking a time-out with your husband? Is it something you feel like you could do? Do you see where there would be a benefit in doing so?

- **Finding a Support Group** – Hopefully you are reading this material as a part of a group experience. If not, know it's critical to have a bevy of women to hold you up and to pour into.

- **Counselor** – I'll just keep repeating this throughout the workbook. Someone that specializes in sexual integrity issues is a must. There are a lot of great counselors out there. If you have any trouble finding one, let me know and I'll do what I can to help you.

- **STD Testing** – If your husband was physically involved with another person, an important part of your own self-care is to get tested for STD's. If you haven't received a proper disclosure or if you aren't sure if your husband is telling you the full truth, it's important to get tested for STD's. This is a very difficult and humbling task to carry out.

One of the gifts that can come out of this difficult process is that more than ever, you have the opportunity to understand yourself better and figure out how you can best take care of yourself. This is vital to your recovery. Nobody else on this planet will do a better job taking care of you than you.

CHAPTER FOUR

Triggers and Needs

Triggers. Are you kidding me? Triggers are the worst. I never knew what a trigger was until my head was barely staying above water in the weeks and months after disclosure. I didn't realize how awful they could be. Navigating through triggers is by far one of the most important pieces of the process. And it's not just wives recovering from betrayal that are triggered. Triggers happen to every person on this planet. But I'd argue that for any wife that is working through a betrayal, triggers take on a whole new debilitating and dreadful residence in her heart and mind.

THE NEUROLOGICAL RESPONSE TO STRESS

When dealing with stressful events, such as triggers, it can be helpful to understand what is taking place in the brain. Let's start with definitions of a couple of the key players when it comes to stress:

- **Prefrontal cortex** – regulates thoughts, actions and emotions; provides insight; when the brain is in a "top down" or non-stressed state, it inhibits inappropriate actions.[20]

- **Amygdala** – involved in the "expression of emotions and emotional learning".[21]

- **Hippocampus** – primarily takes in sensory information and stores it as a memory.[22]

As mentioned a moment ago, in a non-stressed brain, the **prefrontal cortex** serves as the CEO of the brain and when working properly, it exhibits a "top down" control. Simply put, the prefrontal cortex keeps structures like the **amygdala** and **hippocampus** in check.[23]

Unfortunately, the **prefrontal cortex** is also the brain region that is "most sensitive to the detrimental effects of stress."[24] When a stressful condition occurs, there is a "bottom up" regulation where both the **amygdala** and **hippocampus** functions increase and the prefrontal cortex's function decreases. Thus, logic and reasoning go off-line but memory processing and emotional responses increase. This creates a "vicious cycle" where the amygdala function continues to up-regulate all the while the prefrontal cortex's function continues to down-regulate.[25]

We have all experienced these life events (or stressful conditions) that have changed our brains *prior* to disclosure or discovery. These life events, which are negative, hurtful and traumatic change the way our brains function. Specifically, we become susceptible to future events activating old reactions and pain.

Then, disclosure and/or discovery occur which are also very negative, hurtful and traumatic events. Think of the past events plus the disclosure and/or discovery as having a cumulative effect on our brains. This cumulative effect produces a heightened sensitivity and awareness.

When something in our day-to-day life connects to those painful memories, the pain is pronounced and magnified. We aren't just dealing with the present pain but also with the pain from old wounds. This "something" that might set off the painful memories is a trigger.

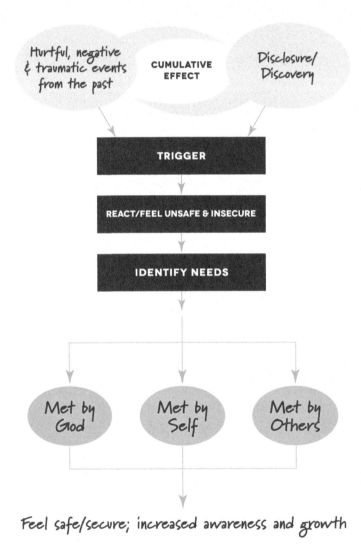

FIGURE 4.1 THE CUMULATIVE EFFECTS THAT PREDISPOSE YOU TO TRIGGERS AND HOW TO GET TO A PLACE OF IMPROVED SAFETY AND SECURITY.

These **triggers** cause us to feel unsafe. They are connected to the past and could be anything – a look, a smell, a gesture, a billboard, literally anything.

Thus, when you encounter a trigger, your brain quickly returns to the memory from the past (although you don't know this consciously), and you go into defense mode and you react. **Reacting is normal yet not ideal.** The reason for this reaction is due to the less desirable "bottom up" regulation explained previously.[26]

You might be feeling hopeless reading the material in this chapter. It seems your brain can be your worst enemy when it comes to triggers. It is painful to react, feel hurt, and lose your sense of reasoning and logic. It definitely feels like your head won't stay above water much longer.

It's important for me to say – triggers don't have to ruin your existence. Nor do you have to assume you are weak because you are triggered. Remember that triggers are normal when dealing with the fall-out of betrayal. Instead of feeling inadequate or broken when you encounter a trigger, let's reframe triggers as something that is both hurtful and helpful. Hurtful because they are painful and decrease your sense of safety. Helpful because they have the potential to:

- **Improve your self-awareness.** Because of triggers, you get the opportunity to ask yourself the hard questions, dig deeper, and ultimately learn more about who you are and how your interactions with others affect yourself.

- **Improve your intimacy with your husband.** As you allow yourself to be more fully known and ask your husband for what you need, you are breaking down the walls you've hidden behind and inviting in authenticity and vulnerability.

- **Improve your relationship with God.** As you ultimately look to Him to speak truth into these fragile pieces of your heart and soul, you will begin to trust God more.

Could it be that at some point you embrace your triggers? Could they be yet another piece of this mess that points you towards healing and wholeness? Maybe. I hope so. And if not, hang on to this: Working through triggers helps the intensity of the trigger diminish and also helps lessen the impact of triggers over time. In addition, research has shown that people who feel in control of their situation (even if this is an illusion) are often not as affected by stress.[27] Thus, know that working through triggers will help you regain control and also help you regain the "top down" regulation that is optimal in your brain.

QUESTION #1 – Think of the last time you were triggered. I asked this question recently on one of my calls and each of us was able to identify a time within the last twenty-four to forty-eight hours. Now that you've identified a recent trigger, think about what you normally do when you are triggered. Write it down.

I asked you to write down how you normally respond because it is important for us to think through how we typically react to triggers. Then ask yourself: is this helpful or hurtful? Complete the table below to help identify some of your reactions to triggers. If you are having trouble identifying how you react, it might help to refer back to this table over the next couple of weeks/months in order to document your reactions.

QUESTION #2 – When I am triggered, what is my typical reaction?

MY **HEALTHY** (HELPFUL) REACTIONS TO TRIGGERS	MY **UNHEALTHY** (HURTFUL) REACTIONS TO TRIGGERS

After we are triggered, in order to get back to a place of safety and security, we must **identify our needs** and pursue getting them met in a healthy way. Keep in mind that you might not even know you are triggered until days later. Once you recognize you have been triggered, it's time to dig in and figure out what you need.

There are three options to choose from in order to meet your needs in a healthy way:

- **A need met by you** – Think of this as something you can fulfill yourself to improve your sense of safety and security.

- **A need met by others** – I refer to this as a "needs request". This is a request we can make to others, primarily our husbands, to improve our sense of safety and security after the fall-out of a trigger.

- **A need met by God** – Sometimes it might be that centering yourself on God's word and engaging in conversation with Him brings you back to a sense of safety and security.

Do not think of having these needs as being "controlling" or "needy". Quite the contrary, for this is an opportunity for you to love yourself well, know what you need and use your voice in order to ask for those needs to get met. It's okay to have needs and it's important that you are able to identify what you need when it comes to triggers. To that end, below is a five-step process to help you work through triggers and identify needs.

FIVE STEP PROCESS FOR WORKING THROUGH TRIGGERS AND IDENTIFYING NEEDS

(*Journey to Healing and Joy* by Marsha Means[28] and *Your Sexually Addicted Spouse* by Barbara Steffens and Marsha Means[29] initially inspired this. See page 36 for an example of a trigger from my life.)

> ***Step One – Identify Potential or Past Triggers.*** What situations remind you of your husband's hurtful behavior? Oftentimes, it is something you see, but it could also be something you hear, a smell, or the way you are touched. Also, remember that the trigger may be directly related to your husband's behavior or it might be more indirect in nature.

Step Two – Identify how this trigger makes you feel and why. For now, refer to the Feelings Wheel (page 141). Once you have worked through chapter seven and chapter nine, you can also refer to the Big Five feelings underneath anger (page 59) and the Three S's (page 76). Also, what is the **why** behind the feeling? Does it connect to something from your childhood? From the betrayal? It could also connect to something else from your past. Explain *why you feel the way you feel.*

Step Three – Identify what you need in order to feel safe. Anything goes here. This is individual and specific to each of us. **Take a moment to focus on yourself.** Think about and write down what you need in order to improve your safety and security.

If you find that you are having trouble coming up with what you need, you aren't alone. This is one of the harder steps. If this is the case, I'd suggest coming up with **a short-term need** (usually related to self-care) that you can do today and continuing to brainstorm about **a long-term need**. Refer to appendix B on page 147 for strategies for healthy self-care that also work for short-term and long-term needs. Keep in mind that you might have to work through several long-term needs before finding a solution. Being a part of a group can be especially helpful here. Loop back to your Go-To Girls and ask for their input on long-term needs for your trigger. Find out what has worked or not worked for them.

Step Four – First, Identify what assistance, if any, your husband can give you in working through the trigger. There are three options. Here is an explanation of each:

- **None** = there is **Nothing** my husband can do about this trigger.

- **Stop** = my husband could assist by **Stopping** this action or behavior in order to improve my sense of security.

- **Start** = my husband could assist by **Starting** this action or behavior in order to Improve my sense of security.

Second, for those applicable to your husband, request your need. Keep in mind that this need might be separate from the need you identified in step three. Remember requesting a need is about inviting your husband into a space to help improve your sense of safety and security. It isn't about punishing your husband. Here are some guidelines to help you through this conversation:

- First, let your husband know that you are working through triggers and at some point you will want to discuss your needs with him.

- Set the tone for the conversation (For instance, give your husband the heads up that you need to talk about your needs related to a trigger. Ask if it's a good time. If now isn't a good time, agree on when you can sit down together and discuss the trigger.)

- Ask your husband if he is willing to allow the conversation to be focused on your needs, not his.

- Use "I" Statements. (For example, "*I feel...*", "*I perceive...*", "*I need...*")

- Make it clear that this is for "my safety and security" and "this is what I need".

- Try to be concise.

- Use a deadline if applicable.

- Marsha Means sums up these requests well when she says that they should be "clean and clear. This means they are honest and vulnerable, direct, non-manipulative, not long and drawn out, fearful, forceful, or controlling in any way. They simply represent what you need, why you need it, and ask the other if they can give it to you."[30]

Step Five – Allow God's truth to speak into the trigger. The final step is to ask God to speak into the trigger. What would He say? What truth does He want to share with you? Quiet yourself. Ask for the Holy Spirit to speak into your soul. Write down the truth He brings to you. Please note – you can use your Bible as a reference but don't feel you always have to attach a scripture to step five.

STEP ONE: IDENTIFY PAST OR POTENTIAL TRIGGER	When Jason walks in the door from work, I haven't seen him all day, and he doesn't look at me or acknowledge me and say "Hello Shelley."
STEP TWO: IDENTIFY HOW THIS TRIGGER MAKES ME FEEL AND WHY	First, I feel insignificant. Then, it scares me because this is "old Jason." This is how he would act when he was in the pit of his addiction and he wouldn't look at me because of his shame. I start to feel unsafe.
STEP THREE: IDENTIFY WHAT I NEED IN ORDER TO FEEL SAFE	I need for Jason to look me in the eyes when he comes home from work. I need him to greet me and touch my arm or my hand.
STEP FOUR: IDENTIFY WHAT ASSISTANCE MY HUSBAND CAN GIVE (NONE, START OR STOP) AND FOR THOSE APPLICABLE TO MY HUSBAND, REQUEST MY NEED	**Start –** Jason could do two things to improve my sense of security. He could look me in the eye when he arrives home and he could touch my arm or my hand. **Need Request -** It went something like this, "Jason, we need to talk. You know when you came in the door a while ago? You didn't look at me or greet me. You went straight to the bedroom. I want to give you the benefit of the doubt that you were in a hurry. And I also need you to know that it triggered me. It reminds me of the past and it reminds me of old Jason. How you used to come in the door and not be able to look at me because of your guilty conscience. I need you to always look at me and greet me when you come in the door. Furthermore, will you place your hand on my arm or my hand when you look me in the eye and say hello? This helps me feel like I am someone that is special to you."
STEP FIVE: ALLOW GOD'S TRUTH TO SPEAK INTO THE TRIGGER	Psalm 139:14 "I praise you because I am fearfully and wonderfully made...." I am significant in God's eyes. He made me "wonderfully".

It is best to complete the five-step process for each trigger before discussing the trigger with your husband. Also, if your husband doesn't appear to be receptive to this part of your process, for your safety, it would be best to discuss these triggers in front of a counselor who specializes in sexual integrity issues.

If your husband acts out, lies, or does something you consider shady; you have every right to not only feel triggered but to also view what he has done as an erosion of trust between the two of you. Chances are, this breach of trust will take the trust rebuilding process back to square one, if not close to it.

However, every time you are triggered doesn't mean that trust between you and your husband is completely eroded. An example would be driving past a triggering billboard or a strip club. You begin to react and remember all the poor choices your husband made in the past. You become angry and tell yourself you will absolutely never trust your husband again. In this example, although it is okay to feel triggered, to react and to feel angry – it's important to remind yourself that your husband hasn't acted out in the here and now. Take a deep breath and work through the five-step process.

PLANNING FOR TRIGGERS

It's also a good idea to plan ahead for triggers. Planning for a trigger is another way you can protect your heart. It may be that you avoid certain areas like women's clothing stores with inappropriately dressed mannequins. Or you might choose not to look at the magazines at the check out line at the grocery store. For myself, early on in the process, my triggers were so out of control that I got to the point where I didn't even want Jason to go shopping with me. Can any of you relate to this? It was easier on me to leave him behind so that I could focus on getting what I needed at the store and not dealing with the fall-out of triggers. I've spoken to women that have reported they don't ever go out with their husbands in public for this very reason. This is understandable early on and I encourage you to give yourself permission to do what feels most comfortable early on in your process. With that being said, know that there will be times when it is best for you to press into your triggers and step slightly outside your comfort zone in order to move past them. In the long term, remember that planning for triggers involves a delicate interplay between self-protection all the while not overly diminishing quality of life.

WHAT DO I DO IF MY HUSBAND ISN'T A SAFE PERSON FOR ME WHEN IT COMES TO PROCESSING TRIGGERS AND ASKING FOR NEEDS?

Working through triggers with our husband's help is definitely the best way for us as wives to move towards healing. But there are times, especially early on in the process, when a wife may feel that her husband isn't safe enough. It's difficult for me to quantify exactly what this might look like. As mentioned previously, if your husband is humble, contrite and broken – chances are, you can press into expressing a needs request. In my experience, a humble and broken heart typically doesn't happen right out of the gate. This is something that takes time and the peeling away of layers before your husband reaches such a place. At least that's the way it was for Jason. If you feel hesitant to express a needs request or to discuss triggers with your husband, I strongly recommend sitting down in front of a counselor (that specializes in sexual integrity issues) to start the triggers discussion and the needs requests you have for your husband.

Remember that expressing a needs request is difficult because you are putting yourself out there and there is a chance your needs will not be met. It's rejection; again. Yet, if you choose to *not* ask for what you need, your husband doesn't have the **opportunity** to *try* to meet your needs. Likewise, if you choose to not ask for what you need; you are choosing out of using your voice and communicating how you feel, what you need and (ultimately) that you matter.

WHAT TO DO IF MY HUSBAND CHOOSES NOT TO COMPLY?

To ask for what you need from your husband, a person that has violated you in such a painful way is a very vulnerable thing to do. It takes a lot of courage to use your voice and express your needs. Knowing that there is a real chance that your husband may say no to your requests makes this all the more difficult.

First, it's important to remember that you can't predict the outcome of the conversation with your husband. To be in control of the outcome of the situation is unrealistic. So from the get go, it's important to focus first and foremost on your needs and the best way to express your needs, leaving the outcome in God's hands.

Second, when your husband chooses not to honor your requests, whether by his words or by his actions, you have every right to feel hurt. When your husband is able to validate your pain, by honoring your needs request, this shows hope. Thus, a wife feels hopeless when her husband won't honor her request. It's okay to express your disappointment and hopelessness to your husband. Not from a standpoint of shaming and belittling but rather from the standpoint of expressing how you feel. Let him know that if he'd like to reconsider or discuss this more, that you are open to this.

Last, take this moment in your recovery as an opportunity to recalibrate and assess your situation. If your husband isn't willing to assist you in feeling safer with triggers, is there a different way to go about it for this season? What can you do to feel safer (step three) regardless of your husband's participation or lack there of? Talk with a trusted friend and/or a counselor. Review your list with them and ask for input. Look to your girlfriends for the support you need that your husband can't give you. It may be that your husband's unwillingness points to the answer you need about his commitment to the marriage. Maybe. If your husband chooses not to help protect your heart, it definitely serves as a red flag.

THE DIFFERENCE BETWEEN A BOUNDARY AND A NEEDS REQUEST

Thus far in this chapter, we have been talking about needs requests related to our triggers. There are also instances where you might need to set boundaries with your husband as a way of protecting yourself when your husband "acts out". You may need to institute boundaries at the point of disclosure or discovery, or it may be sometime afterwards when you realize what you need. We will discuss boundaries and an array of boundary options in the next chapter. For now, it's important to point out that a **needs request** is typically something we use to invite our husbands to stop or start doing in order to **improve** our sense of security. Think of needs requests as being related to triggers. On the other hand, typically a **boundary** is something we use in order to **protect** ourselves from further hurt, fear, anxiety and insecurity. It's not necessarily that we are being triggered but rather we know we need to implement certain boundaries to protect ourselves from being hurt further. And last, keep in mind that boundaries and needs requests are not always distinct and separate - there is definitely some overlap. So try not to get too caught up in the semantics. Boundaries and needs requests go hand in hand in certain situations

STAYING AFLOAT

Dealing with triggers is key in your recovery. Triggers don't necessarily ever go away but they will ease as you move forward on your individual journey, so it's important that you learn how to handle them effectively. I encourage you to start taking notes of your past triggers, current triggers and triggers that might come up in the future. Start working through them using the five-step process discussed earlier; the chart is below. Refer to appendix C for an extra chart. In addition, visit rlforwomen.com/resources for a printable version. Plan to share one of your triggers in the next group session or with one of your Go-To Girls. Preferably, it would be a trigger that you are having trouble working through.

STEP ONE:
IDENTIFY PAST OR
POTENTIAL TRIGGER

STEP TWO:
IDENTIFY HOW THIS
TRIGGER MAKES ME
FEEL AND WHY

STEP THREE:
IDENTIFY WHAT I NEED
IN ORDER TO FEEL SAFE

STEP FOUR:
IDENTIFY WHAT
ASSISTANCE MY
HUSBAND CAN GIVE
(NONE, START OR
STOP) AND FOR THOSE
APPLICABLE TO MY
HUSBAND, REQUEST
MY NEED

STEP FIVE:
ALLOW GOD'S TRUTH
TO SPEAK INTO THE
TRIGGER

CHAPTER FIVE

Boundaries

As mentioned in the previous chapter, a boundary is something we put into place to **protect** ourselves from unnecessary hurt, pain and anxiety. Remember the words *protection* and *self-respect* when thinking about boundaries. You may also think of boundaries as a guardrail or fence around your heart and soul. Keep in mind that boundaries are not walls. Rather, think of them as a fence with a gate. In this way, the boundary is able to breathe - it keeps out the bad and lets in the good.[31] Consider a woman with healthy boundaries; it might be that her heart has a low fence with a gap between the boards. Her gate is closed, but unlocked. And now consider a woman with no boundaries or very little boundaries, she might have a couple of fence posts unsteadily planted in sand. She has very little boards between the fence posts and her gate is wide open. And last, on the other end of the spectrum is the woman with walls. She wouldn't dare let anything in or out in an effort to protect her self. She does a great job at keeping out all the bad, but at a high cost. She is missing out on anything good that might come in. Keep these visuals in mind as you work through this chapter.

OWNING YOUR VOICE AND IDENTIFYING YOUR FEELINGS

One of the many hard pieces of this process is using your voice to set boundaries. I believe for most wives, at the point of disclosure and/or discovery, we are in a place of feeling both voiceless and experiencing feelings-confusion. Feelings-Confusion - a word I just made up - simply means not being able to pinpoint the feelings within. You may also want to think of this as not having a lot of self-intimacy or fully knowing yourself. **One of the first steps in my road to healing was finding my voice and finding my feelings.** Setting boundaries would have come much easier for me if I had already developed these parts of my character. What I noticed is, over time, there became a synergy between setting boundaries and using my voice/identifying my feelings. In other words, setting boundaries actually helped me find my voice and identify my feelings and needs. And as I was able to find my voice and identify my feelings, it became easier for me to set boundaries.

In more recent years, it's been important for me to understand why I started this process feeling voiceless and experiencing feelings-confusion. Here are a couple of thoughts:

- In my family of origin, I perceived my feelings and needs to be inconsequential. The result, in effect, was my thoughts; opinions and needs went out the door. I didn't know how to say no and instead made sure that everyone else's needs around me were met. I was voiceless.

- When married to a man with a sexual integrity issue or a sexual addiction, manipulation is at play. As Jason used manipulation to get what he wanted and to hide his behaviors, oftentimes I became more voiceless and confused with my feelings.

- Piggy-backing off of the last point, I felt like maybe I was cRaZy while Jason was in the throes of his addiction. The craziness caused me to wonder: "Do I even have the right to have feelings?"

- It doesn't help that some have taken scriptures like Ephesians 5:22-24 to the extreme and you think you must submit to your husband no matter his behavior. I know for myself, in the early days of our marriage, there was a constant struggle between submitting to Jason and deep down feeling like there was something terribly wrong. Confusion around my role led to confusion about my feelings and a misunderstanding of what it meant to have a voice.

- When it came to dealing with the pain of betrayal in my marriage, it seemed easier to deny my feelings in order to protect myself.

QUESTION #1 - Now I'd like for you to take time to think through why you might feel voiceless or experience feelings-confusion (if applicable). For example, were you validated for how you felt in the home you grew up in? Do you have a history of putting others needs and feelings before your own? Journal about this below.

If any of the thoughts above resonate with you, remember that insight is powerful. Once you recognize and put words to what is going on within, you can start to take steps towards healing. To that end, here are two quick things that helped me early in my process. My counselor repeated these two phrases over and over to me and thus I repeated them to myself over and over and over again (and guess what, I still do!):

- "It's not my fault. There is nothing I could do to prevent Jason from coping with pain through a sexual addiction."

- "I get to feel however I feel. There is no feeling that is wrong. I will own my feelings."

THE TRUTH ABOUT BOUNDARIES

As you prepare to set boundaries with your husband, I want to make sure that you know the truth about these fences. Refer to table 5.1 for common misconceptions and the truth.

COMMON **MISCONCEPTIONS** ABOUT BOUNDARIES...	**TRUTH** ABOUT BOUNDARIES...
Boundaries are used to punish my husband.	Boundaries are used as a healthy way to protect others and myself.
Boundaries should only affect my husband.	Boundaries that I implement will affect many people including our children and myself.
I wouldn't have to use boundaries if I wasn't in relationship with an addict.	Boundaries are healthy borders that we should all use in every relationship.
I'm controlling when I set boundaries.	I am loving myself and accepting my needs and my desire for safety when I set boundaries.
Setting boundaries is simple.	Just checking to see if you were paying attention. Boundaries are complicated. Especially when it comes to being firm with boundaries, knowing what to do when they aren't respected and knowing when it is okay to release them. On the other hand, sometimes boundaries can be as simple as saying "no". Keep in mind that with practice, boundaries have the potential to become easier.
Boundaries will make my husband change.	Boundaries do cause discomfort and might accelerate the process, but choosing to change is between your husband and God.

TABLE 5.1 COMMON MISCONCEPTIONS AND THE TRUTH ABOUT BOUNDARIES.

QUESTION #2 – Which of these misconceptions have you believed to be true and why?

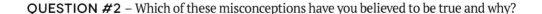

DEVELOPING AND SETTING BOUNDARIES STARTS WITH SOLID GROUND

I've read that in order to effectively set boundaries with others, you must first be in a secure relationship with someone else (including God) **that will love you no matter what.**[32] These secure relationships keep you grounded and provide an attachment which you need before you can develop and set boundaries. Think of it this way, just as a fence post won't remain stable in two inches of sand out in the middle of nowhere with a gale-force wind blowing through; nor will a boundary work when a wife doesn't have the support she needs from a safe group of people that love her just as she is and will not abandon her. If you are involved in a support group or have a group of women that love you through your ups and downs – first, thank God. Then, know you are on stable ground. You can set your fence posts in two feet of earth surrounded by concrete in the most quiet and serene place. The post will remain stable as you start to develop and set your boundaries.

QUESTION #3 – Do you have a group of Go-To Girls? These would be ladies that know your every thing. They've seen your ugly. And they've seen your good. (Psst... If you are using this material as a part of a support group – you're in luck. Your Go-To Girls are a phone call away!) You know that they will stand by you through the good and the bad. If your answer is no, what steps do you think you need to take to find these Go-To Gals? Is there anyone in your life right now that you feel you could invite into a more deep and intentional relationship with you? If you are at a loss for a group of girls to connect with, please contact me and I can help you find that group.

And just a little encouragement for you here, know that it was after several failed attempts that I believe God brought me my Go-To Gals. We meet every other week and pour our hearts out to one another. It's been one of the greatest gifts God has given me over the last decade. Keep searching for your girls. They're out there. And when you find them, it will revolutionize your life!

Refer to appendix D on page 151 for a list of tools to help build your fence and gate. Remember, we are focusing on letting the good in and keeping the bad out. Use the list either for specific ideas or as inspiration to create the boundaries that you uniquely need. Keep in mind that one of the benefits of setting boundaries is that it gives your husband an opportunity to begin rebuilding trust.

BOUNDARIES AND SACRIFICE

As you start to think through what sort of boundaries you might need to put into place, keep in mind that boundaries require sacrifice on your part as well. If, for instance, you ask that your husband attend couples counseling with you weekly – know that this will be a sacrifice of both time and finances for you, too. Another example, if you request an out of house separation – understand that this will be a sacrifice for you in numerous ways. Remember, there is a balance between implementing boundaries that provide enough protection to feel safe, while not punishing yourself in the process.

WHEN MY HUSBAND CHOOSES NOT TO RESPECT MY BOUNDARIES

For those of you that have husbands that respect your boundaries, your fence might look similar to the fence described at the beginning of this chapter: a low fence with gaps between the boards and an unlocked gate. However, if your husband consistently disrespects your boundaries or continues to break them, your fence will look different. Not only might your fence be taller and the space between the boards smaller but your gate might also be locked. Furthermore, it might be that you set your fence even further away from your heart, ensuring that you are protected.

In one of my first groups that I facilitated, I witnessed as a wife delicately and beautifully held to her boundaries. As her husband continued to not respect them, she slowly moved her fence further and further away; giving herself more and more room to breathe. It started with an in-house separation, then an out-of-house separation. She was open and hoping for her husband to come to his senses and she was ready and willing to let his good in. At the same time, she moved forward with her life. She continued to work on herself and protect herself. She played that delicate dance of setting boundaries to protect her heart and hoping for her husband to change; yet not waiting around for him to change. While focusing on herself, she has since changed careers, moved across the country to be closer to her children, and purchased a home all on her own. Although she has not divorced her husband, she has exhausted all other options while waiting for him to show change. Today, she believes that divorce could be her final step since she hasn't seen any change in him.

LIVING IN THE GRAY

In the book entitled Shattered Vows, author Debra Laaser makes a great point when she talks about boundaries and how we, as wives, navigate enforcing our boundaries. She says it's okay to live in the "gray". We don't necessarily have to communicate a bottom-line to our husband's on the front end or the back end of a boundary. What I mean is, you don't have to say up front what the consequence will be if the boundary is broken. Instead, you can share with your husband that you aren't sure what you will do if/when the boundary is broken, but what you do know is: **you choose not to live like this anymore**. Debra goes on to say that living in the gray allows you the space to adjust and tweak as you move forward in your individual processes.[33]

With this in mind, it's okay to not know exactly what you will do if your husband chooses not to comply. There is no magic formula. It doesn't mean you give in. Similar to triggers, it means you reassess. You reach out for support. You adjust your game plan. It also means you start to take steps away if boundaries continue to be broken.

HOW DO I KNOW IF IT'S TIME TO REMOVE A BOUNDARY?

Time frames, when it comes to boundaries, are very dependent on the boundary as well as each couple's situation. Working with a counselor can definitely help when it comes to forming and implementing boundaries as well as to know when the boundary is ready to be removed. Trust me, solid counseling is worth the investment.

Here are a couple of questions to help guide you as you start to think about potentially removing a boundary:

- Is my husband contrite and humble?

- Has he made gains in his recovery (not through his words but rather by his actions)?

- Is my husband living with integrity (both sexually and otherwise)? Is he living honestly?

- Is my husband not acting in a defensive manner?

- Do I feel safer? (Think of this in regards to why the boundary was initially put into place.)

If the answer is "yes" to these questions, it might be that a boundary can be lifted. Maybe. Again, knowing when to remove a boundary is difficult to put into words.

It's also worth mentioning, as you begin to trust yourself again – including how you feel and what you think - that you listen to your gut. Sometimes you know that you know that you know that you need to enforce a boundary. And sometimes you just know that it's time to lift a boundary. For myself, some of the boundaries slowly started to lift as my safety and trust increased in Jason. As for the reason my safety and trust was increasing – well, it was because of all the hard work Jason was doing and all the change I started to see in him. But there were some boundaries that didn't lift so naturally. If you are feeling significant reluctance to lift a boundary, know that you are not alone. Some boundaries can be a leap of faith to lift. Centering yourself on trusting and depending on God is critical when lifting the ones that don't naturally fall away.

STAYING AFLOAT

Remember that establishing boundaries in relationships is of huge importance. It might be that before now, you haven't had a lot of practice at setting boundaries. Working through this process well help refine your boundary setting skills. It will also keep you sane. Think of boundaries as yet another tool that will aid in your rescue.

CHAPTER SIX
The Grieving Process

Elizabeth Kubler-Ross is the woman responsible for developing the five stages of grieving. She wrote a book entitled *Of Death and Dying* where she described the stages people go through at the end of their life before they die. In a lot of ways, this discovery of your husband's sexual integrity issue is like a death. A death of what you *thought* your marriage was. A death of a dream, a death of whom this man is you thought you knew, and for some wives there's a little girl inside whose dream of 'happily ever after' has died.

Before we dig into each stage, it's important to clarify a couple of things regarding the grieving cycle. First, remember that the grieving process isn't linear but rather cyclical. You will continue to cycle through the grieving process for days, months and even years. In addition, you may cycle through stages concurrently or within the same day. It feels like you have taken a ride on the cRaZy train. Remind yourself that this is normal and part of the necessary work to move forward. Below are the five stages of the grieving process plus an explanation.

THE GRIEF PROCESS

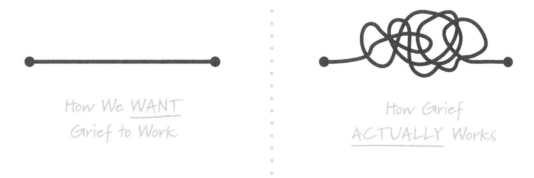

How We WANT Grief to Work

How Grief ACTUALLY Works

TABLE 6.1 WHAT WE WANT GRIEF TO LOOK LIKE VERSUS WHAT IT REALLY LOOKS LIKE.

DENIAL/SHOCK: I love what Melody Beattie says about this stage. She says denial isn't lying...it's the shock absorber for your soul."[34] What this means is, your mind naturally protects you in the initial days and weeks after you are confronted with a stressor, which in this case, is your husband's sexual integrity issue. The denial helps you continue to function and move forward as you start to integrate this new stressor into your life.

Keep in mind that for some wives, it's tempting to stay in denial and not acknowledge the truth of the situation. If you think this may be you, one of the best things I've found to help me move forward is to start to process the information. Whether by journaling, talking to a trusted friend or spending dedicated time engaging the reality of your situation – processing the information can help you move forward in the process. At the same time, this can be tricky. Because you are dealing with trauma, you need to be careful not to re-traumatize yourself by talking about it over and over and over again. Finding the right balance is critical and this looks different for every woman.

ANGER: We all know what it feels like to be angry. I think the difficult part of anger is expressing it in a healthy way and also being able to move past it. Anger is a real, valid, and necessary emotion. It's a fire alarm for our heart and soul. This alarm signals that there are feelings and emotions underneath the anger that must be addressed. My husband, Jason, refers to these feelings and emotions as the "Big Five". And what he typically sees is our anger points to an underlying feeling of **hurt, fear, failure, shame and/or disappointment.** By working through the anger and addressing the feelings underneath, you are able to move forward in the grieving process and not get stuck. We will discuss this more in the next chapter.

BARGAINING: As mentioned earlier, the grieving process isn't necessarily linear. So bargaining may present it self amidst one of the other stages. As you begin to move towards acceptance of your reality, there are still moments where you start to bargain. Here are a couple of examples of what bargaining can look like:

- *"It's okay if my husband doesn't change, I will just wait until my children are grown and out of the house and then I will do something about this."*

- *"If he continues to look at pornography, I guess I can make it. As long as my husband doesn't have an affair with another woman. I will be okay as long as that doesn't happen."*

- *"You know, he really is a good person otherwise. He may not be faithful to me but he really is a good dad and a good person."*

- *"Why did I marry him? Why didn't I know? Why would God let this happen? If only I could _____, it would be okay."*

Bargaining may be your soul's way of taking a deep breath. You aren't experiencing the intense anger when you are parked here. But you also aren't quite ready to encounter the space known as hopelessness.

DEPRESSION / HOPELESSNESS: This stage, in my opinion, is one of the most difficult stages because this is the stage when you finally feel the pain and devastation of your situation deep in your bones. Some say this stage begins when you begin to humbly surrender.[35] This is when you are at your lowest and grieving your situation in full. You may feel hopeless, you may feel sad; there will definitely be a lot of tears. More than anything, you are finally looking at your situation through a lens of reality, not of denial. And yet, there is also a sweet peace that comes when you start to surrender to God and accept your situation. You begin to fully trust in Him. You find your strength in Him. You accept your situation.

Which brings us to the last stage of the grieving process: **ACCEPTANCE**. Words to describe this phase include freedom and peace. Acceptance doesn't necessarily mean that you agree with or are content with your situation. You merely identify it as your reality and learn to cope with a "new normal", regardless of whether you are with your husband or without him. It's also common to accept certain parts of the reality while working towards full acceptance of the entirety of your new situation.

Although I've read that this stage is void of feelings, and isn't necessarily a stage that is wrought with happiness, I tend to disagree. I think that for a Christian woman, full acceptance of your situation can bring other gifts that you didn't even know were waiting for you around the corner. True forgiveness, a new trust paradigm, emotional intimacy, and a deeper understanding of who you are and who God made you to be, to name a few.

QUESTION #1: Which stage of the grieving process do you feel like you are currently sitting in?

QUESTION #2: Name some of the things you have lost during this process. Are these permanent losses or temporary? Have you grieved these losses?

STAYING AFLOAT

Keep in mind that the grieving process is cyclical, not linear. It is typical to continue to cycle through the grieving process for a long time, and quite possibly, forever. My friend Maggie helped me realize this a couple of years ago when she told me she will probably never stop grieving the loss of her mother. Sure, the grieving looks different as the months and years roll by, but she believes it is a loss she will always grieve. As you move forward in life, you will encounter moments that remind you of where you've been. For Maggie, this occurred with the birth of her first child, Lillian. Maggie felt the hurt and loss of her mom's death on a different level and the grieving continued where she left off. In Maggie's words, "Time doesn't necessarily heal all wounds. It makes our wounds look different. Only true healing comes from God."

The same could be true for some of you with what your husband has done. You might continue to grieve your reality especially as life throws you curve balls and celebrations. So, it's important to remember that if you find yourself angry or hopeless all over again, it isn't that you didn't do it right the first time. Rather, you simply have more grieving to do.

CHAPTER SEVEN

Anger

For anyone who chooses to engage this process, there are multiple life-long benefits you can take with you. One benefit is that you are given the opportunity to work through some really difficult emotions, like anger. It will serve you well to understand anger better and to be able to use it in a positive way not only in regards to the situation with your husband, but in other areas of life.

Remember that anger is a natural part of the grieving process. Anger is a real and valid emotion. Think of it as a fire alarm for your heart and soul. This alarm signals that there are feelings that must be addressed.

QUESTION #1: What is your perception of anger? Do you feel it is all right to express anger? Do you believe anger is a sin?

Every wife feels the emotion of anger. And each of us deals with it differently; a lot of this difference is dependent upon the acceptance (or not) of emotions, including anger, in our families of origin. It's safe to bet that most of us didn't learn to deal with anger in a healthy way (or maybe it's just me?). When it isn't dealt with in a healthy way, it typically seeps out in one of two unhealthy ways:

- **Anger Submarine** - Some wives were taught to not express anger. Expressing this emotion is viewed as sinful or wrong. In addition, to express anger would be vulnerable and increase your risk of rejection. So instead of letting out your anger, it seeps out, for instance, in a passive aggressive way. (This is also known as implosive anger.)

- **Anger Wall** - Others were taught that anger was acceptable, but any feelings underneath anger (like sadness or fear) were not acceptable. In this way, anger is used as a protective wall to preclude any sort of meaningful intimacy. (This anger is known as explosive anger.)

QUESTION #2: Which type of anger, anger submarine or anger wall, did you see modeled by your parents or other people close to you when you were a child?

QUESTION #3: Which type of anger do you tend to gravitate towards?

QUESTION #4: Have you found it difficult to be vulnerable with your husband and express anger towards him? If so, why?

QUESTION #5: Do you relate to some wives that have used anger as a protective wall to preclude meaningful intimacy? If so, why?

What I hope for you is that through this material and with practice, you can land somewhere in between the anger submarine and the anger wall; a healthy place where you are able to use anger to move yourself forward in the healing process. A place where you can be true to yourself and express your anger and also uncover the emotions underneath.

ANGER 101

In order for you to give anger a chance at working to your advantage during this process, let's consider it from a couple of angles. Let's start with the definition of anger. Gary Chapman, well known for his concept of the five love languages, defines anger as a **response** "that arises whenever you encounter what you perceive to be wrong."[36] It originates from the Latin word "angere" which means, "to strangle". It's important to note that when you become angry, it's yet to be determined if there has been a wrongdoing. In other words, just because you are angry does not mean that someone has done something wrong. Initially, it's just our perception of a situation that has caused you to become angry. Chapman goes on to explain the purpose of anger. He says when you encounter injustice; anger is designed to motivate you to take action in a loving and positive way with an end result of leaving things better than how you found them.[37] I don't know about you, but when I feel angry there doesn't seem to be much love or positivity about it and in fact, I can think of anger as the opposite of love. When you feel love towards someone, you want to draw closer to him or her. When you feel anger towards someone, you are against him or her.[38] But I do think Chapman makes a great point. When you feel angry, the intent isn't to destroy your husband but rather to use anger *as a motivator to leave things better than the way you found them.*

Another angle on anger, I came across while reading the book entitled *Boundaries*. The authors state that anger is a boundary. It helps you distinguish your perceptions as different from someone else's. Cloud and Townsend go on to say that for children that are able to appropriately express anger, later in life, they will recognize their anger as alerting them to the fact that someone is trying to hurt them.[39] I appreciate this view of anger because it helps validate the hurt. You have the right to feel really angry about what your husband has chosen to do. His choices have hurt you. Your anger alerts you to this.

ANGER IN THE BIBLE

Let's also consider anger from a Biblical perspective. We find that the word "anger" is used in the Bible 234 times and the word "angry" is used forty-four times.[40] We also see that not only were people angry with each other but also with God. Consider the well-known story of Jonah. In brief, Jonah was a Jewish prophet that God called to preach to the city of Ninevah. Jonah ran away and eventually landed in the belly of a fish for three days and three nights. During this time, Jonah prayed a heartfelt prayer and the fish "vomited Jonah onto dry land" (Jonah 2:10). God gave Jonah a second chance to go to Ninevah and this second time, Jonah obeyed. It took Jonah three days to go through the city proclaiming what God asked him to say: "Forty more days and Ninevah will be overthrown (Jonah 3:4)." And amazingly, the people repented. We find in Jonah 3:10 that "God relented and did not bring on them the destruction he had threatened."

Now that you have a little back-story, we will focus on the fourth chapter of Jonah. Jonah, an Israelite, becomes angry with God for having compassion on the people of Ninevah. As a side note, Jonah was probably so angry because the Ninevites were terrible people; they killed Israelites. It's as if God sent him to preach to his enemies. The Hebrew word for anger in Jonah 4:1 is charah, which literally means in this passage the "burning of anger."[41] The Bible often describes anger in terms of heat. Think of anger as a fire shooting up from your heart. It's your warning that there is an issue you need to confront.[42] Jonah prays a second prayer and at this point asks God to take his life. It's important to note that the original text shows a *setumah*, which means there is a brief pause before continuing.[43] It's as if God is taking a deep breath before responding. Then God asks Jonah a question. He says: *"Is it right for you to be angry (Jonah 4:4)?"*

I'd like to point out that a lot of people have a view of Jonah as being a self-centered and whiny man. I hope to show you a different perspective through some key take-aways.

There are three things that you can learn from Jonah and apply to yourself with respect to anger.

- First, God is both patient and loving towards Jonah. He didn't roll his eyes. He didn't walk away. Instead, He allowed Jonah to vent. The same applies to you. It is okay for you to be angry in regards to your situation as well as feeling angry with God. God is big enough to handle your anger.

- Second, Jonah was real with God. He was vulnerable to allow God to see that he was frustrated, disappointed and angry. This can be so difficult because of the possibility of rejection. But did God reject Jonah? Absolutely not. The take home here is you can be completely vulnerable and real with God and trust that He will not reject you.

- Third, God asked Jonah a very valid and practical question, *"Do you have the right to be angry?"* One that you can in turn ask yourself when you start to feel the discomfort of anger –God was asking Jonah "to examine his heart and see why he was really angry."[44] Try not to get hung up on if it's okay to be angry or not. Anger is a feeling that deserves your attention (versus resorting to anger submarine or the anger wall). A lot of times, you have no control over feeling angry. What it means is there is something that needs to be addressed and worked through. So what I'd like for you to dwell on is **examining your heart and figuring out exactly *why* you are angry.**

David writes about this examining of ones heart in Psalm 4:4-5 when he says "Don't sin by letting anger control you. Think about it overnight and remain silent. Offer sacrifices in the right spirit and trust the LORD" (NLT). Clearly, David is encouraging his followers as to the necessary steps to take when dealing with anger. First, to not sin. Second, to think about it by taking an inventory of the heart versus pointing out sin in others.[45] Here is the point, from both Jonah and David, remember that it is okay to feel angry and to be honest and vulnerable about the anger you feel. Furthermore, when you recognize you are angry, it serves as a prompt to take a heart inventory and figure out exactly why you feel angry.

Now that you better understand what anger is for, you can start to think about how to get angry for good. You can begin to implement healthier ways of dealing with anger and thus use it to help propel yourself forward in your healing.

TAKING A HEART INVENTORY

So what might it look like to take an inventory of your heart? Below are several suggestions:

- ***Asking for Wisdom*** - You can go before God and ask him to give you wisdom about the emotions you are feeling. James 1:5 says "If any of you lacks wisdom, you should ask God, who gives generously to all without finding fault, and it will be given to you." In this passage, James was specifically writing about what to do when faced with a difficult situation (see vs. 2-4). It's through asking for wisdom that you are able to grow from your trials and also better "understand how to use these circumstances for your good and God's glory."[46]

- ***Process it Out Loud*** - I think it is also helpful for me to talk it out with a trusted friend. Start the conversation with saying, "I need to vent. Can you just listen to me and wait until I am done to give me feedback?" Another option is to ask the person to not give you feedback. A lot of times when Jason and I vent to each other, we ask if this is a "fix it" or "listen" conversation. And the one of us that is venting gets to decide...do I want the other to fix it (as in, give feedback), listen (as in, no feedback), or both.

- ***The Big Five*** - As mentioned briefly in chapter six, underneath our anger is typically one of five emotions: *hurt, fear, failure, shame* and *disappointment*. These are called the "Big Five". It's important for you to always ask yourself what emotions are underneath the emotion of anger. Yep, it's back to self-intimacy. By recognizing the feelings underneath the anger, you are able to move forward because you can appropriately respond to them and identify your needs. Thus, your needs actually have a chance to get met.

Think about what it looks like when a toddler gets angry. They scream, they cry, they writhe on the floor. And at some point, they get it all out and they are calm. My counselor once told me, we should learn from toddlers. Somewhere between childhood and adulthood, we stop letting our anger out in a healthy and constructive way. Although there are several methods for letting out anger (hitting a pillow, screaming into your hands and kicking the air), the tool we will use together to let out anger is an anger letter.

Find a quiet place where you can devote your entire self to this project. Make sure there are no distractions. Write a letter to your husband. You may also want to write one to the other woman/women he devoted his sexual energy to. (See page 62 for space to write the letter/s.) These letter/s aren't for the recipient to view. As you write, try to get out as much of your anger as possible. Write about the fact that you are angry. Write down all the reasons that you feel angry. Write about what the anger feels like as it smolders inside of you. Take note of what you have lost because of this anger. Try to allow yourself to write as much as you need to with absolutely no filter.

Once you have written this letter, think about how you feel. Do you feel any relief? Do you feel more rage? Hold onto the letter and you will have the opportunity to read the letter to your group in the next session. (As a side note, I know it might seem scary to read your anger letter aloud. From my experience, there is an even deeper level of release from verbally sharing my letter within my group.)

DISCUSSING ANGER WITH YOUR HUSBAND

It's important that you work towards being forthright with your husband regarding your anger. Ephesians 4:25-27 says "Therefore each of you must put off falsehood and speak truthfully to your neighbor, for we are all members of one body. In your anger, do not sin. Do not let the sun go down while you are still angry." "Put off falsehood" literally refers to the masks that were worn in Greek theatre.[47] What Paul is saying is to not pretend like you aren't angry but rather to be authentic and vulnerable and take off your mask and discuss your anger. When you are able to let your husband in and show your true emotions, you are practicing self-intimacy. This is how you can leave things better than the way you found them.

Depending on your situation and dynamics with your husband, it may work best to start discussing this anger while sitting in front of a counselor. Use your own best judgment as to how this should be handled.

Refer to table 7.1 below for a summary for working through anger in a healthy way.

RECOGNIZE YOU ARE ANGRY	Consciously acknowledge to yourself that you are angry. "I am angry about this, now what am I going to do?"[48] Just as Jonah was real with God, let's practice being real with God and ourselves.
LET OUT SOME STEAM	It's therapeutic to let out the anger in a constructive and healthy way. I've experienced much relief from getting my anger out.
INVITE GOD IN	This is the beginning of the heart assessment. Ask God for wisdom as you continue to process your anger. Psalm 37:3 says, "Be still before the LORD and wait patiently for Him." Just as God was patient with Jonah, He will be patient with you.
TAKE A HEART INVENTORY	God asked Jonah to examine his heart and figure out *why* he was angry. Ask yourself this question as well.
WHAT IS THE UNDERLYING EMOTION BENEATH THE ANGER?	You are continuing the heart assessment here. Remember the "Big Five", hurt, fear, failure, shame and disappointment.
DISCUSS YOUR ANGER WITH YOUR HUSBAND	This is where you get to practice being emotionally intimate and vulnerable with your husband, discussing your anger in a loving and authentic way.
WORK TOWARDS EXTENDING FORGIVENESS AND GRACE	I will discuss forgiveness further in the next chapter. For now, remember that forgiveness is a gift you give yourself. By extending forgiveness to your husband and to others, you slowly start to heal the wounds in your heart.

TABLE 7.1 SUMMARY FOR WORKING THROUGH ANGER IN A HEALTHY WAY.

Remember that working through anger is a process. It takes time, energy and intentionality to sit down and start to uncover all the layers of emotions underneath it. Refer to table 7.1 as you start to move through this process. And remember, you aren't alone in your anger. Invite a trusted friend, counselor or your support group in as you start to acknowledge your anger and work through it in a healthy way. Last, keep in mind that anger is a conduit for leaving things better than the way you found them. It takes you one step closer towards healing and wholeness.

ANGER LETTER

Date: _____   Time: _____   To: _____

CHAPTER EIGHT
Forgiveness

If you are expecting to hear about how "you need to forgive your husband right now" and "oh, by the way, forget as soon as possible"; you're reading the wrong workbook. Sit back and relax. Take a deep breath.

Ladies, I have been in your shoes. I too have wondered: *"is it truly possible to forgive him?"* I was aware of the fact that forgiveness was important. I also knew I was commanded to forgive. But I didn't know that my heart would *ever* be in a place of complete grace and forgiveness toward Jason.

WHAT FORGIVENESS IS AND WHAT FORGIVENESS IS NOT

I find a lot of times when I am discussing forgiveness with wives, there are a lot of misconceptions about the choice to forgive. For instance, some wives feel like if they forgive their husbands, then they should be able to trust their husband. Some wives think forgiving means they have no right to bring up the past or to be angry about what has happened. It seems a lot of husbands believe this, too; but it's simply not living in reality.

QUESTION #1: Take a moment to consider what *you* believe about forgiveness, regardless of whether it is true or not. Write it down.

Here in a bit, we will come back to what forgiveness is and what forgiveness is not. For now, let's look at what Biblical forgiveness looks like.

As you start to think through what forgiveness looks like from God's perspective, it's important to look to His word for insight and guidance. Use table 8.1 to review several key verses related to forgiveness.

KEY VERSE	COMMENTARY
Ephesians 4:31-32 *"Get rid of all bitterness, rage and anger, brawling and slander, along with every form of malice. Be kind and compassionate to one another, forgiving each other, just as in Christ God forgave you."*	One of our great motivators in forgiving our husbands is because God forgives us.
Isaiah 1:18 (NKJV) *"Come now, let us reason together, says the LORD: though your sins are like scarlet, they shall be as white as snow; though they are red like crimson, they shall become like wool."*	Not only are we given the opportunity to forgive others throughout this process but we are also given a greater appreciation for how we've been forgiven, through Jesus' death and resurrection.
Matthew 18:21-22 *"Then Peter came to Jesus and asked, "Lord, how many times shall I forgive someone who sins against me? Up to seven times?" Jesus answered, "I tell you, not seven times, but seventy-seven times."*	We will discuss this verse in full. For now, know that this verse points out that forgiveness is a limitless and active process.

TABLE 8.1 KEY VERSES RELATED TO FORGIVENESS FOLLOWED BY COMMENTARY.

Let's take the passage from Matthew 18 and discuss it further to learn more about what forgiveness looks like from a Biblical perspective.

THE PARABLE OF THE UNMERCIFUL SERVANT

(You may read Matthew 18: 21-27 although these verses are paraphrased below.)

As you look at verse 21, it's important to note that some people think Peter thought he was being generous in offering to forgive seven times. Keep in mind that Rabbis in that day instructed people to forgive a total of three times.[49] Peter is basically saying, "I'll double the standard and raise you 1". Perhaps he was expecting a high-five from Jesus for being so spiritual.

Jesus corrects Peter in the number of times he should forgive someone; seventy times seven. He then shares a parable with Peter and the others gathered. In this parable, Jesus talks about a servant and his master (a king). One particular servant was brought to the king who owed him ten thousand bags of gold. (In Greek, "ten thousand bags of gold" is translated as "ten thousand talents". One talent was worth about twenty years of a day laborer's wages.[50]) Since the servant was unable to repay the king, the king ordered the servant, his family and all he owned sold in order to repay the debt. The servant begs for the king to be patient with him and he promises to pay everything back. The king chooses to forgive the servant and cancel all his debt and ultimately lets him go. The parable continues but I'd like to stop and point out several things.

First, the Greek word here for forgiveness is "aphiemi" literally translated as "to let go, to give up a debt". I appreciate the words "to let go". I imagine my hands opening wide. Slowly. And whatever I'm holding so tightly falls. I imagine this in slow motion. It takes volition to do this. Intentionality. It is active. Just as God lets go of our transgressions, we are instructed to do the same with our husband's transgressions. Forgiveness is the only way to level the playing field. When your husband held on to his secret sin, hiding his addiction from you; there was no way you could experience true intimacy with him. Same with un-forgiveness – when you choose to hold onto the hurt, it creates a distance in the marriage that precludes true intimacy. It's only through forgiveness that the relationship can continue to be restored.

Second, let's look at the word "seven" and the words "seventy times seven" (or seventy-seven times). Historically, the number seven carries a lot of significance from a religious perspective. The number seven was thought of as "perfect" and "complete". For instance, the seven days to complete creation. Maybe this is why Peter used this number; he thought that forgiving his neighbor seven times would mean complete forgiveness. The Greek word for the number "seventy times" is indicative of the absence of any limit. It points to the idea of being "limitless". Jesus used this number to point Peter away from a numerical standard. Just as God's forgiveness is limitless, so should be the same with our forgiveness towards our husband.[51][52] What this tells us is: **forgiveness is a limitless process**. Paula Rinehardt speaks eloquently to this when she says, "Forgiveness is both an event and a process". It's one big yes "followed by many little yeses as the months and years roll by."[53]

Third, It would have been impossible for the servant in this parable to repay his master. He would have had to work about 200,000 years in order to repay the debt. This is an example that shows the heart of forgiveness. When you extend forgiveness to someone, just as when God extends forgiveness to you, not only is there nothing expected in return but there is also no possible way the wrong-doer can make things right. The same applies to the situation with your husband. **Your husband simply**

cannot make up for the damage done. There is no way he can repay you. When you forgive, you are cancelling the debt since it cannot be repaid.

Taking what you have learned thus far, below is a quick reference to what forgiveness is as well as what forgiveness is not.

FORGIVENESS IS…	• For you. • The cancelling of a debt. • Releasing someone from the wrongs they have committed. • An active, limitless and intentional process. • A choice, not necessarily a feeling. • Freedom. • Restoring peace to an otherwise turbulent soul.[54] • Levels the playing field.
FORGIVENESS IS NOT…	• For your Husband. • Forgetting. • Saying that what someone did is right or okay in your eyes. • Usually a one-time action. • Based on your emotions. • Giving up protection or saying the pain is gone or the healing is complete. • Doesn't necessarily mean reconciliation. • Keeping track.

TABLE 8.2 QUICK REFERENCE TO WHAT FORGIVENESS IS/FORGIVENESS IS NOT

A GUIDE TO FORGIVING OUR HUSBANDS

One of my favorite authors these days is Kelly Minter. In her book, *The Fitting Room*, she compares the process of forgiveness to dissecting an artichoke. She discusses the difficulty of getting to the heart of the artichoke. It involves "whittling away at the pointy leaves" and the "peeling away of layers".[55] It is a long and arduous process, peeling back so much before getting to the heart of forgiveness.

Keep in mind that the forgiveness process is similar to the grieving process in that it is more cyclical than linear. You might experience more than one of these phases on a given day. You might move backwards before moving forwards again. Thus, instead of using the word "step", call these different pieces of forgiveness "phases".

PHASE ONE – OWNING YOUR FEELINGS AND SITTING IN THEM

We discussed in chapter three the importance of self-intimacy. Being in touch with yourself is the first step in the forgiveness process. We also learned in the last chapter the importance of taking a heart inventory to see if there is any anger that needs to be dealt with.

QUESTION #2: Do you feel bitterness or resentment towards your husband? If yes, describe how that is expressed.

As you allow yourself to feel these feelings and work through them, you start the process of "whittling" away at the "pointy leaves", so that you can ultimately uncover the beautiful heart that God has in store for you. Working through these feelings via an anger letter, as we discussed in chapter seven, is an important and necessary step towards forgiveness.

PHASE TWO – RECOGNIZING THE NEED TO FORGIVE

Once you are able to be honest with yourself about the bitterness or resentment you are feeling in your heart it opens the door to the reality that choosing to forgive is in your future.

PHASE THREE – RECOGNIZE THAT FORGIVENESS IS A PROCESS

As you are doing this, don't forget the story in Matthew:

> Matthew 18:21-22 "Then Peter came to Jesus and asked, "Lord, how many times shall I forgive someone who sins against me? Up to seven times?" Jesus answered, "I tell you, not seven times, but seventy-seven times."

Forgiving your husband isn't a close-the-door-and-walk-away kind of forgiveness. This is a continue-to-forgive kind of forgiveness for as long as it takes. I think of the artichoke; each "pointy leaf" represents a multitude of times that I forgive. In other words, sometimes you forgive for the exact same thing multiple times. And sometimes your forgiveness occurs in stages... ("I can forgive *this* today, but not *that*.")

PHASE FOUR – UNDERSTAND THAT GOD IS A FORGIVING GOD AND THAT FORGIVENESS IS SUPERNATURAL

Alexander Pope once said "To err is human, to forgive divine." Something supernatural occurs when you choose to forgive. You take the leap of faith. You let go of the hurt. You let go of the control. And you gain something you can't comprehend: peace in your heart. I'll never forget the day I finally took that leap of faith and gave my big "yes" to God and thus forgave Jason. It was truly a Kairos moment, which is defined as a unique and special moment in time when heaven and earth collide with each other in a spiritual sense. Even though I wasn't sure what would happen, God was faithful and took care of the rest. And don't get me wrong, it wasn't a one and done; but God closed the gap between my selfish human desire to not forgive Jason and my heavenly soul that knew it was time to let it all go. As I look back on this forgiveness process, I have a deeper sense of appreciation for those that forgive me and for the gap that Jesus filled in my life when he was crucified on the cross.

PHASE FIVE – COMMUNICATE FORGIVENESS

In my experience, there was never a time that I felt like forgiving Jason. But, I knew when the Holy Spirit was pushing me to do it. It's as if there were flashing arrows pointed towards "It's time to release and allow freedom in" everywhere I turned.

QUESTION #2: Have you sensed God asking you to forgive your husband? If so, in what ways have you sensed this?

Once you feel God pressing you to forgive, it's time to take action and communicate your forgiveness. I'm going to outline a couple of different options on how to go about this part of the process. You may choose one of these or you may sense God asking you to do it a different way:

> **Option One** - Write a letter to your husband and be specific about what you are forgiving him for. Take your time writing this letter. I spent almost an entire day working on my forgiveness letter to Jason. Read this letter to your husband. Time-stamp the letter so that you know the day you said your big "yes". This is important because I know for myself, it wasn't forty-eight hours before I was second-guessing, *"Did I really forgive him?"*

> At some point, when you are ready, I recommend writing a letter to anyone else you need to forgive. Examples include your husband's mistress, women in pornographic media, co-conspirators, etc. It's important to note that most often, these forgiveness letters will never be sent. You can tear them up into shreds, perform a ceremonial burning, or file them away as I did. Just make sure if you destroy these letters to write in your journal the date you forgave these people.

> **Option Two** – Purchase a glass vase and small rocks from a craft store. Make a running list of the things you need to forgive your husband for in your journal. When you are ready to forgive your husband for a particular indiscretion on your list, write a word on the rock to remind you of the offense. Lift up a prayer for the indiscretion and place the rock in the vase. Take your time and continue to do the above until you've worked through all the items on your list.[56]

QUESTION #3: Which of these forgiveness options sounds do-able to you? Or is there a different option that God is pressing on your heart to use?

PHASE SIX – CONTINUE TO FORGIVE

I hope one of the things you've taken from this chapter is the fact that forgiveness never ends. Once you choose to forgive your husband, the battle isn't over. You get to choose to continue to forgive him each passing day. In *Strong Women, Soft Hearts*, Paula talks about a semi-annual ritual she performs. She removes herself from all distractions and takes out a pen and legal pad. She asks God to bring to mind anyone that she is bitter toward. She begins to journal about her feelings. She lets go of the pain they have caused and she extends forgiveness to them. I'm so inspired by this ritual. What a lovely way to do a heart cleanse.

Below are four questions that I'm often asked in regards to forgiveness:

Question: So how do I know when I have forgiven my husband?
Answer: You can check your heart and ask yourself the following questions:

1. Is there a negative emotional charge when I think about him?

2. Am I experiencing bitter thoughts towards him?

3. Do I feel superior towards him?

4. Do I feel he still owes me?

If your answer is yes to any of these questions, there still may be more forgiveness work for you to do. Remember, forgiveness is an active process. Think of it like this: it might be that you have forgiven your husband. And when you feel a negative emotional charge about his choices, it's time to forgive him again.

Question: Does my husband need to give me a full disclosure in order to forgive?
Answer: The quick answer is no. It's your husband's choice to come clean with you and if he doesn't give you a full disclosure, you will still have forgiveness work to do. However, when your husband has shown you the courtesy and respect to give you a full disclosure, you are able to extend a more authentic and real forgiveness. This was most certainly the case for me. Initially, Jason told me very little of the truth. I quickly forgave him and nine months later found myself even more bitter and resentful toward him. When Jason finally chose to give me a full disclosure, I felt like I was able to more fully process the indiscretions and authentically forgive him.

Question: Is there a time-line I should follow for forgiving my husband? My pastor told me that everything would be better if I would just forgive him. If I do that, then he said we could move on.

Answer: There is absolutely no time line when it comes to forgiveness. Yet I do have an opinion: Forgiving quickly is not something I would recommend. As mentioned in the last answer, I tried it that way. I quickly forgave Jason and realized I was just trying to put salve in my wound. It didn't work.

In addition, once you forgive your husband, the process is not over. From my experience, I can tell you that forgiveness was a turning point for me and for us. However, there have been years and years of processing, grieving and working toward full reconciliation and healing within my marriage after I gave my big yes of forgiveness.

Question: How do I forgive my husband when he isn't repentant? He doesn't always act like he is sorry, I don't see a contrite and broken spirit, and he continues to hurt me by acting out and/or breaking boundaries. He partly blames our problems on the fact that I can't forgive him and move on.
Answer: I'm going to answer this question in three parts.

Part One – Remember that forgiveness is primarily a gift you give yourself. Sure, your marriage and your husband can benefit from forgiveness but this is a secondary benefit. Second, remember that forgiveness doesn't mean reconciliation. When he states that he wishes you could forgive and just move on, it sounds like what he is really saying is, "let's reconcile." Furthermore, "let's move on and forget that any of this ever happened." Although forgiveness does include "letting go" of the resentment you feel and removing your husband as a prisoner in your heart, it definitely doesn't imply reconciliation and forgetting it ever happened isn't living in reality. Forgiveness can be one step closer to reconciliation but the two are not synonymous. Also, no matter the situation, nobody moves on as if nothing happened. Your life is changed forever. And if your husband continues to act out, it becomes even more important for things NOT to return to the way they were.

Part Two – In my opinion, *receiving* forgiveness from a wife is quite difficult when her husband isn't sorry. In fact, some think that repentance and sorrow is a prerequisite to receiving forgiveness.[57] In other words, only when your husband acknowledges how deeply he has hurt you can **he** fully receive your forgiveness. If your husband doesn't "feel" like he has been forgiven, that is on him, not on you.

Part Three - It's worth mentioning that forgiveness is just plain hard and I think **it is much harder to forgive someone that isn't asking for forgiveness and continues to hurt you compared to a husband that is sorry, contrite, humble and doing whatever it costs to repair the damage done.** I appreciate what Lewis Smedes says in his book, *The Art of Forgiving*, in regards to forgiving those that aren't repentant. He says "forgiving unrepentant people is a no-lose opportunity – difficult to do but with a harvest of healing" awaiting.[58]

Remember that forgiveness is an active process. It's not a one and done. It's a big moment in time followed by little moments until you get to heaven. Forgiving your husband will probably be the most difficult forgiveness you will ever work through. And there are so many benefits waiting: peace, freedom, and self-respect to name a few. Not to mention a deeper appreciation for God's forgiveness toward you. Remember that forgiveness isn't something to be rushed nor pressured into. My prayer is that with God as your guide, you will be obedient to His prompting to extend forgiveness to your husband.

CHAPTER NINE
Recognizing the Holes in your Heart

A lot of our unhealthy behaviors are driven by holes in our hearts that we desire to fill. Unfortunately, we all learn how to fill these holes in a temporary way through "doing". I will explain this more here in a bit. The long-term goal is to start to fill these holes in our hearts in a healthy way. The first step in this process is to name the holes. So let's get started.

THE THREE I'S

Jason teaches a concept to his clients known as the Three I's. The concept is as follows: we are all born with holes in our heart that only God and the Body of Christ can fill. In addition, through negative experiences in our upbringing, these holes can grow wider. The easiest way to grasp what the three I's mean is to consider the questions behind them. Think of these three I's not only as feelings but also as self-concepts (see table 9.1).

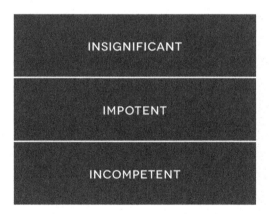

INSIGNIFICANT	"Do I matter?" "Do I have value or worth?"
IMPOTENT	"Do I have power or control?" "Can I affect change?"
INCOMPETENT	"Am I good enough?" "Do I have what it takes?"

TABLE 9.1 THE THREE I'S AND THE QUESTIONS THEY ANSWER.

I was reviewing this information with a colleague and dear friend of mine. She proposed to me that there is a more specific "female version" of the Three I's. I'm going to call them the Three S's.[59]

THE THREE S'S

Just like the Three I's, the Three S's are holes in our hearts that we are all born with. They have the potential to grow larger through negative life experiences from childhood and beyond. It's through our relationship with Jesus and the Body of Christ that we can start to fill these holes. Refer to table 9.2 for the questions behind them.

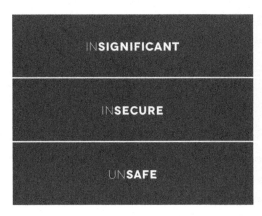

IN**SIGNIFICANT**	"Do I matter?" "Do I have value or worth?"
IN**SECURE**	"Am I okay just as I am?" "Am I grounded?"
UN**SAFE**	"Can I be vulnerable and transparent?" "Do I feel protected?"

TABLE 9.2 THE THREE S'S AND THE QUESTIONS THEY ANSWER.

As I've mulled this over, I believe that for women, significance, security and safety are self-concepts that are very close to the heart. We all desire to see ourselves as significant and secure and we desire to feel safe. I know for myself, these self-concepts are at the top of the list. However, keep in mind that this doesn't mean that the Three I's don't apply; because they still can and do at times. It might just be that you find you gravitate more towards the Three S's.

I believe that it's because of these holes in our hearts (insecurity, insignificance and lack of safety) that also makes sexual betrayal so painful. We will have a chance towards the end of the chapter to explore this further.

PROCESSING YOUR HURT AND NAMING THE I/S

Typically, when you are hurt by another person, whether intentional or not, it activates one of the three S's. It can be very helpful if you are able to name it and claim it. What I mean is, when you are specifically able to say how you feel and why, you can move forward in the process of healing from your hurts in a healthy way.

On the other hand, when we don't have the self-intimacy and insight to recognize when one of the Three S's is activated, we have a greater propensity to numb the pain versus dealing with the raw emotions and needs underneath the pain. Again, simply naming how you feel can move you forward in your individual process. This is exactly what leads to the addictive and compulsive issues your husband has struggled (or currently struggles) with in terms of his sexual integrity. When your husband "acts out", he feels significant, powerful and/or competent which is medicative for the pain and feelings he has chosen not to deal with. Thus, it's not about sex and it's not because of a deficiency in you. It's about what sex is providing for your husband (for him to feel and see himself as significant, powerful and competent). It's taking a good thing and making it an ultimate thing. The same applies to you. What you use as coping mechanisms typically taps into one of the three S's. It's through your coping mechanisms that you feel more significant and secure as well as safer.

Last year was my oldest son's kindergarten year and let me tell you – something about having my baby in school really triggered my insecurities from childhood. A lot of what upset me had to do with the Three S's being pricked deep within my soul. As I mentioned earlier, it doesn't necessarily have to be intentional. For instance, when I would hear of a little boy from Truman's class having a birthday party that Tru wasn't invited to, it would bother me. I would feel a pang of hurt. Left unchecked, knowing myself, I'd start to medicate in some unhealthy way. I'd find comfort through food, start to withdraw and push others away in self-protection, or start to self-criticize and come up with reasons to justify the non-invite.

I have to tell you, I feel vulnerable sharing about this insecurity. I also know the truth; we are hurting people. It's normal to feel hurt by others (whether someone deliberately tries to hurt us or purely by happenstance). A lot of times, we, as women think something is wrong with us if we can't rise above. Do better. Be better. Instead of being so hard on ourselves, let's take the time to dig in, figure out why we feel hurt and accept our selves right in the middle of it.

QUESTION #1: Think about a recent time you were hurt by someone and share a little bit about it here.

QUESTION #2: Next, which of the Three S's was activated when you think about that hurt? And why did you feel this way?

A person who finds their identity by "Being" is someone that is self-confident and okay with exactly the way God made them. They understand that a loving God made them uniquely and wonderfully. There is nobody else on the planet like them. And this is a good thing. "Doing" describes someone that isn't okay with the way God made them. They think they need to "do" things in order to be significant, secure and safe. They look to this world to fill those holes in their hearts. Whether through changing their body image, excelling in their career, making more money, buying more things, or through befriending the "right" people (to name a few).

Back to my example, I want you to know that initially, I felt hurt for myself and for my son. Why wasn't he invited to the party? I spent time thinking through what was wrong with me or wrong with him. I started the mental process of trying to figure out what I could "do" in order to make sure this didn't happen again. It may seem sad, but I seriously thought maybe we should finish our landscape project so that we could socialize more (because we all know, in order to socialize, the backyard has to be perfect?!). Maybe Tru needed to have more play dates. I could go on and on with what we needed to "do".

QUESTION #3: What are some things you "*do*" in order to feel significant, secure and safe? (Hint: refer to questions one and two and think through what you "did" in order to feel significant, secure and safe.)

Think about how much energy "doing" takes. From your answer above, circle the things that you feel may come between you and your relationship with God. For example, which of the activities fulfill you in a way that you know is a substitute for God's fulfillment?

To close the gap on my example, what I ultimately did was I sat down and identified which of the Three S's was activated when Truman wasn't invited to a party. Underneath that hurt, I felt insignificant. Did my son (and thus myself) matter? I also felt insecure. Is Truman (and thus myself) okay just as he is?

It was after processing my hurt and identifying what was activated that I was able to speak truth to myself. We didn't need to change ourselves (or our yard for that matter!). It's a reality of life - not always being included. In addition, practicing covering those lies we hear in our heads with God's truth (which we will discuss in detail in the next chapter) can help us start to fill those holes in our hearts.

APPLYING WHAT YOU'VE LEARNED TO YOUR PRESENT SITUATION

I want you to be able to apply the concept of the Three S's to all areas of your life. Hence, the reason for the birthday party example with my oldest son. It's also important to be able to apply this to your situation specifically with your husband. Thus, I'd like to give you one more example from myself specifically related to Jason's betrayal.

Nine months before I confronted Jason and demanded he tell me the truth about a particular relationship, Jason came to me and dribbled out just a little bit of his ugly truth. Jason refused to process this new information with me. I was devastated. Heartbroken. Utterly confused. It ripped open new and old wounds in my heart. Let me explain how it impacted the three S's:

- **InSignificance** – I had never been "chosen" by a boy until I met Jason. This was a wound of mine that I didn't even know I owned but was carrying around with me. Needless to say, I felt completely unchosen and insignificant when Jason shared a hint of what was going on in his secret world. I thought Jason only had eyes for me, but on that fateful evening in Frisco, Texas, I realized that wasn't the truth. My husband had eyes for other women, too. I didn't feel like Jason's chosen bride; I felt disposable. All of these feelings point towards the wound of insignificance.

- **InSecure** – I decided that it was my fault that Jason was interested in other women. I wasn't very sexy. And he convinced me this was a big issue. I decided that I needed to change who I was in order to save my marriage. It was obvious that who I was wasn't working. I went out and purchased some sexy apparel. I decided I needed to have sex with Jason as much as possible. I was anything but grounded in my self-security.

- **UnSafe** – I felt incredibly unsafe after Jason's confession. I started to reach out in old patterns to feel protection. In particular, I started working more and I started restricting my food intake, all in an effort to feel some sort of protection over my new reality.

Now let's apply the three S's to your present situation. How has your husband's betrayal tapped into the Three S's?

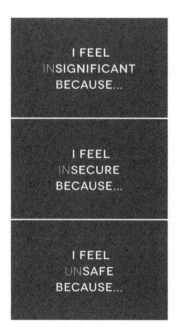

As you start to unpack how the betrayal has opened or reopened these wounds, it's also important to identify things you might "do" in order to try to fill the gap.

QUESTION #4: What are you "doing" in order to fill the gaping holes from the pain and devastation of your husband's betrayal? (This could look similar or different than your answer to question three.)

Working through these wounds has taken years. God is still using this pain to bring me new insight and practice filling these holes through my relationship with Jesus versus through "doing". In addition, because of the work I have done in this area, I've been able to more quickly process interactions, like the birthday party, that tap into the Three S's.

STAYING AFLOAT

Having a grasp of the Three S's and filtering your hurts through them is a technique you can use to help yourself process your pain and move forward in a healthy way. Keep in mind that at the end of the day, it's through your relationship with Jesus that you are free to simply "be". Rest easy in that. Refer to table 9.3 on the next page and use the verses to start practicing filling yourself with God's truth.

INSIGNIFICANCE	"Do I matter?" "Do I have value or worth?"	**John 15:16** "You did not choose me but I chose you and appointed you so that you might go and bear fruit – fruit that will last…" **Ephesians 2:10** "For we are God's hand-iwork, created in Christ Jesus to do good works, which God prepared in advance for us to do." **Psalm 139 vs 4, 13, 14** "Before a word is on my tongue, you, Lord, know it completely", "For you created my inmost being; you knit me together in my mother's womb", "I praise you because I am fearfully and wonderfully made…" **Psalm 56:8** "You've kept track of my every toss and turn through the sleepless nights, each tear entered in your ledger, each ache written in your book" (MSG).
INSECURE	"Am I okay just as I am?" "Am I grounded?"	**Psalm 40:1-2** "I waited patiently for the LORD; he turned to me and heard my cry. He lifted me out of the slimy pit, out of the mud and mire; he set my feet on a rock and gave me a firm place to stand." **Isaiah 43:1-2** "…Do not fear, for I have redeemed you; I have summoned you by name; you are mine. When you pass through the waters, I will be with you; and when you pass through the rivers, they will not sweep over you. When you walk through the fire, you will not be burned; the flames will not set you ablaze."
UNSAFE	"Can I be vulnerable and transparent?" "Do I feel protected?"	**Exodus 13:21-22** "By day the LORD went ahead of them in a pillar of cloud to guide them on their way and by night in a pillar of fire to give them light, so that they could travel by day or night. Neither the pillar of cloud by day nor the pillar of fire by night left its place in front of the people." **Psalm 37:23-24** "The LORD makes firm the steps of those who delight in him; though they stumble, they will not fall, for the LORD upholds them with his hand." **Psalm 18:28-29** "You, LORD, keep my lamp burning; my God turns my darkness into light. With your help, I can advance against a troop; with my God I can scale a wall."

TABLE 9.3 COVERING THE LIES IN GOD'S TRUTH

CHAPTER TEN

Wounds, Lies and Truth

One of many things I've had to come to terms with as an adult is the fact that I was wounded as a little girl. This isn't a dig on how I was parented. In fact, my parents did a lot of hard and intentional work when it came to how they chose to raise my brothers and me. We live in a fallen world and wounds are a reality none of us can escape. As I look back on my life, I realize that at a young age, I learned how to cover up my wounds. It seems we all do this to a certain extent. We hide our wounds, allowing them to incubate and not receive healing, which eventually leads to a false sense of self. We end up wearing masks. Usually, we have no idea we are even doing it. In the end, not only are we hiding who we really are from each other, but we are also hiding who we really are from ourselves.

Let's take one of the examples I shared from the last chapter. When Jason came to me and opened the door slightly into his secret world and quasi-confessed one of his hurtful actions, it devastated me. I was confused and wanted to ask questions, but Jason made it clear when he said, "what's in the past will stay in the past. Let's move forward" It was obvious that my questions weren't going to be answered. I accepted his response and internalized all the pain. The **lie** floating around in my head was that I wasn't good enough. I wasn't sexy enough. I wasn't sexy enough to keep my husband faithful to me. This lie circled in my head for a long while. At some point down the road, I made an **agreement** that the only way I would be able to keep my husband was to become sexy. I **vowed** to become a sexy person in how I dressed and in how I acted. This eventually led to a **false sense of self**. I wasn't being Shelley, I was trying to be what I saw in a Victoria's Secret catalog. And in this process, I lost a piece of who I was and how God made just me and only me.

A huge part of our restorative journey is taking these wounds both from our past and our present and allowing them to heal versus allowing them to fester and cause destruction in our lives. Often the hurt from the betrayal is an opportunity for us to examine other wounds (from both past and present) and begin our healing.

To explain this process and more clearly define the steps that take us from a wound to a false sense of self, I've adapted a model (Table 10.1) found in the book entitled *Surrendering the Secret*.[60]

	EXPLANATION OF:	EXAMPLES INCLUDE:
WOUNDS	Wounds can occur early in life. We live in a fallen world and the reality is we will endure hurt and pain. Nobody is immune to wounds.	Sexual infidelity, feeling unloved or unchosen as a child, abandonment or not feeling wanted, miscarriage, trauma, abuse, death, etc.
LIES OR FALSE BELIEFS	These wounds become contaminated with lies. Think of the lie as the way we justify our pain and hurt in our mind. It is the beginning of our efforts to reconcile the hurt, with an overall goal of not feeling the pain and possibly also a way to have some control over the pain/hurt.	"I'm a mess-up" "This is all my fault" "I'm stupid" "Nobody wants me." "Nobody cares about me" "If I were ____ this wouldn't have happened"
AGREEMENTS	That little voice in our head (Satan), repeats the lie over and over until we agree with the lie and accept it as truth. We then make the agreement and **accept the lie.**	"This is what I deserve" "Life isn't perfect, this is just how it is." "I can't live without it." "I must change who I am in order to save my marriage."
VOWS	Once we make agreements, a vow is soon to follow. This is our **promise of how we will do life differently in order to not get hurt again.**	"I will never again..." "From now on I will always..." "I will only trust myself."
FALSE SELF	This is the **mask** we now wear based on the domino effect of the wound, lies, agreements and vows. **The ultimate lie.**	Think of this mask as a lens we use to view the world. This mask informs the choices we make. It also ensures the world sees us a certain way.

TABLE 10.1 MODEL OF HOW OUR WOUNDS CAN LEAD TO A FALSE SENSE OF SELF.

APPLICATION: Think of a wound from your life, both an event from childhood as well as a recent wound specifically related to your husband's betrayal. Please note, these can be two completely separate wounds. Use the table below to show how each wound slowly led to a false sense of self.

	EXAMPLE FROM SHELLEY'S CHILDHOOD	EXAMPLE FROM BETRAYAL OF SHELLEY'S HUSBAND	EXAMPLE FROM MY CHILDHOOD	EXAMPLE FROM THE BETRAYAL OF MY HUSBAND
WOUND	The embarrassment of never having a date to homecoming; living in my brother's shadow; being called "fatty" and "ugly".	Jason chose other women over me before and during our marriage.		
LIE	"I'm not acceptable the way God made me." "I'm an ugly duckling." "I'm unchosen."	"I can't trust anyone. Certainly not Jason. And certainly not God. If He allowed this to happen, what else might he allow to happen to me?"		
AGREEMENT	"I can't change my face, so I will have to change my body."	"Well, this is just how life is. Each woman for herself."		
VOW	"I will never gain weight or else people won't accept me."	"I will never again trust anyone, including God."		
FALSE SENSE OF SELF - THE MASK WE WEAR.	Frail, thin girl that starved herself. My security was found in my body image versus in the truth that God loves me, I'm protected by God, and secure because of God.	Young woman that self-protected by keeping everyone at a distance. I thought this was an okay way to live but the truth was, I was missing out on intimate relationships by keeping everyone, including God, at a distance.		

QUESTION #1: How can you stop this cycle of allowing your wounds to ultimately influence you enough to wear a self-protective mask?

Here are some strategies to help you work toward living in truth versus wearing a mask:

- **Sharing your story** with women that you trust and that are willing to speak truth into your life (a healthy support group is the best place to start).

- **Confessing your shortcomings to God and to others.** This takes being real and vulnerable. I used to think I needed to be perfect, to have it all together. By way of example, Jason has shown me what it looks like to mess up, admit it, and move forward in freedom. I've found that when I confess and agree with my shortcomings, I'm not alone. Others relate. Others say "me too."[61] This is freedom. (And by the way, as I'm sitting here typing this out, Jason is behind me working on his computer. I just heard him say, "Okay. I messed up." {I'm so not kidding!} Freedom, people. Freedom.)

- **Cover the lies in God's truth** (see the table on page 83).

- **Prayer** – Asking God to give you the wisdom and discernment to hear the voice of truth.

- **Counseling** – Towards the end of a recent session with my counselor, she told me something profound. She said, "A lot of what I'm trying to do is help you listen to the voice of truth within yourself." If this is an area that you are struggling greatly with, seeing a wise counselor will be worth the investment.

- **Being proactive, intentional and self-aware.**

- **Gratitude Journal** – This is a great tool to use to help retrain your brain to see the blessings and the good in each day.

As you go about the week, be aware of the things you tell yourself. Write them down below. Of the things you tell yourself, what are the lies? What is truth? If you have trouble distinguishing between the two, share what you've written with your group. Let them help sort out what is true and what is false. Use the table on page 87 to work through the lies you hear. For instance, you may know what the lie is but you may not know the wound. Or you may know the vow you have made but not anything else. When this is the case, work your way both up and down the table until you have a clear picture of how the wound led you to a false sense of self.

Use the space below to write down the things you tell yourself this week. For the things you say to yourself that are lies, write out next to it what the truth is. Try to start replacing the lie you hear with the truth you know.

LIES	TRUTH

CHAPTER ELEVEN

Moving Beyond Insecurity

Jason and I are on a flight from Orange County back to Denver. We spent three nights in Laguna Beach - mostly relaxing - but also speaking at a small conference. Throughout the course of the weekend, I couldn't get over the differences between Denver and Laguna. You may think that I'd mention the palm trees (versus pine trees) or the ocean (versus mountains). But that's not the case. Two things constantly reminded me that I wasn't in Denver: the fancy cars and the women. I'll focus on the women here and leave the cars for another day.

Over the first couple of days, I felt myself becoming more and more insecure. I started to question my looks. Here are a couple of the thoughts that were floating around in my mind:

- *"We could never live here. I couldn't stand for Jason to always see these beautiful women."*

- *"Wow, she is really thin. I guess I could take better care of myself: eat less, run more; and maybe I could look like that, too."*

- *"I can't compete with these women. It's unfair. They've had plastic surgery. I haven't."*

Our last full day in Laguna, as I mentioned earlier, we were to speak to a group gathered at the hotel. I remember getting out of the shower and feeling insecure about my body. I think it was a combination of the delicious food we had been eating over the past forty-eight hours and the self-comparisons between me and these other women. Not to mention the devil's scheme to thwart me from the important work God had given us for the day.

I stopped myself, and said the following: *"Shelley, you are beautifully and wonderfully made. Nobody cares what you look like. What they care about is your heart and what flows from it. Put these insecurities aside. And go do what God has asked you to do."*

I spoke truth to myself. I covered the lies in God's truth.

And I also realized: as women that have been betrayed by their spouse, it's important that we spend some time focusing on security. Insecurity in our culture is pervasive. And I believe that when women are betrayed, insecurity is taken to a whole new level.

QUESTION #1: In what areas have you felt insecure as a woman? Think childhood, early adulthood, pre-disclosure as well as today.

QUESTION #2: After you were faced with the truth of your husband's indiscretions, were there any new areas of insecurity and/or areas from question #1 that became more magnified?

FIVE PRACTICAL WAYS TO WORK THROUGH INSECURITIES

Insecurity has been a topic often brought up in my support group. To that end, about two years ago, a couple of us read the book *So Long Insecurity* by Beth Moore. Towards the end of the book was a gold mine. Beth gives four practical ways that we can work through our insecurities.[62] They are so good that I want to share them with you here. I've added a bonus fifth one!

1. **Stop Making Comparisons**

Beth makes a compelling argument that typically when we compare ourselves to others, we are comparing whatever it is that we hold most valuable. For instance, during all the years of my active eating disorder, I would enter a room and (I cringe to admit this), assess each and every woman and see if any of them were thinner than me. If I were the thinnest, my pride would erupt. And if I was not the thinnest, I felt like a failure. It's in these moments of life that I'm reminded of the seven words Theodore Roosevelt strung together so profoundly and eloquently. He said, "Comparison is the thief of all joy."

QUESTION #3: What about you? Have you ever walked into a room and compared yourself to others? If so, what measuring stick did you use? (It might be related to clothing, size, hair color, skin, etc.)

There are **three things** we can do to stop comparing ourselves to others. **First, is to simply recognize that we are doing this.** I'm not always aware of the comparison reel playing in my head. It's only after we gain the insight to listen to that small, negative, pull-me-down voice that we can do something about it. **Second, choose to use this opportunity to replace the lies with the truth.** It might be a breath prayer that you say to yourself anytime you are comparing yourself to others. An example would be: *"I am fearfully and wonderfully made."* Or it might be reciting a Bible verse that speaks to your soul. Use the table on page 83 as a starting point. **And third, embrace your individual uniqueness.** Beth mentions a verse that speaks perfectly to this. It's Galatians 5:26 and it says this, "We will not compare ourselves with each other as if one of us is better and another worse. We have far more interesting things to do with our lives. Each of us is an original" (MSG).

QUESTION #4: Take some time to think through what makes you unique. What gifts and passions did God give you that are unique to you? Use the space below to journal what comes to mind.

QUESTION #5: As you look over your list, which of these unique attributes have you stifled or hidden from others? Are there any qualities that you feel you need to embrace and show to the world?

Whenever you choose thankfulness for the individualities that God has given you, you begin to rest in a place of God-centered confidence. This, like so much else, is an active process. It doesn't come easy. It won't happen overnight.

For example, I used to want my freckles to go away. I thought if I tanned, maybe all my freckles would blend together into one big freckle. It never worked. I also really wanted to have my two best friends' gorgeous long and thick hair. The only thing that helped my hair thicken up was pregnancy and as much as I love my boys, I think I'll pass on any more pregnancies. Honestly, girls, it's been in the last couple of years that I've started to be at peace with my freckles and with my hair. Actually being *thankful* for my unique qualities is still something I'm working on.

2. Start Personalizing Other Women

Although Beth uses this concept to discuss personalizing other women that may not pose a threat, I'd like to focus your attention on how you can use this concept to help soften your heart to the "other" women. Know that as you read this, if you feel you aren't ready to personalize the other woman/women, that's okay. Give yourself a pass and revisit this at another point in time. It took me years, I mean *years* to get to a place where I could extend grace to these ladies. When you are ready, know that personalizing these women can be a huge game-changer.

Not only have I compared myself to the women Jason used but I also vilified them. In some respects, this vilification can be justified. But in the end, it does me no good. Remembering that there is a "why" behind what the other woman wears or how she acts towards men allows me to start to personalize them. For instance, there is a reason that they are willing to show a little more cleavage in order to get attention from men (and by the way, wearing revealing clothing, showing more cleavage, etc. is not a prerequisite to be the "other" woman). There is a reason that Jason found them as an easy target. Maybe they were abused as a little girl. Maybe they didn't have a father figure in their life. Maybe another man hurt them. It's then that my heart begins to soften and I begin to replace the vilification with grace. In no way am I excusing the other woman's behavior. But when I view the other woman as a broken person, just as I am; and when I come to grips with the fact that I am about three poor choices away from being in the same boat as this other woman, I am able to decrease the amount of power they hold over myself.

3. Don't Trip Another Woman's Insecurity Switch

This is all about being humble and respectful to the men and women that you are surrounded by. It's about stopping yourself and making sure that you aren't motivated to wear something or act a certain way because you feel insecure and want to attract attention. Nobody understands this more than a wife that has been betrayed. There is an incredible sensitivity in the early stages of this process to how other women are acting as well as what they are wearing. It isn't that you can take away this sensitivity in others but you can work towards being more aware of others and not wearing inappropriate apparel or behaving in a manner that might make another woman uncomfortable.

QUESTION #6: I realize that this is subjective to a certain extent, but take some time to think through a situation in your life that you feel you could choose to be more diligent about what you wear or how you come across to both men and women.

4.   **We Must Be Examples of Secure Women**

Basically, we could start a revolution. By becoming secure women, we can show others in tangible ways what this looks like. And this could start a redemptive ripple effect. Who knows how far-reaching your impact could be. It CAN start with you.

5.   **Being Intentional To Encourage Your Friends**

Words are powerful. As you get to know women on a deeper level, you begin to see their unique qualities and individuality. No need to keep your words a secret. Be intentional to communicate to your friends what you see in them that is a God-given uniqueness. Celebrate what you observe with your friends. It can be a benefit both to you and your friend to affirm her special design.

IS IT INSECURITY? OR IS IT A TRIGGER?

As I've continued to work through my insecurities, I've found that there are times when I'm not sure if what I'm experiencing is a trigger or an insecurity. What I've realized is that the two co-mingle. To that end, here are a couple of helpful hints as you continue to navigate this often times tricky process of working through insecurities. **First, awareness is key.** The more I practice self-awareness and dig deep when I start to feel those familiar feelings of hurt and inadequacy; the better I am able to name what I'm experiencing as insecurity. I've found that when I can name what I'm feeling and what is going on inside of me, the more peace I have and the more clarity I have to move forward with the process. **Second**, I've found that when I feel insecure, **using the five-step process to work through triggers, found in chapter four, has proved helpful.** Specifically, I've found it's important to identify how the insecurity I'm feeling as an adult relates to my past.

It seems when my insecurity switch is flipped, I start to react and my levelheaded thinking flies out the window (like I said, this insecurity stuff really reminds me of triggers). Once I take a breath and a step away from the situation, I start to speak truth to myself. Here is a recent excerpt from my journal:

02/13/2015

Truth:

- I don't need to be the most beautiful or the most perfect woman to have friends, love life, have joy or be used by God.

- God made me as he saw fit. He is the author of my life. I choose today to love me. To love my freckles. To love my wayward hair. To love my eyes even when sensitive and red. To love my small lips. To love each and every wrinkle because I've earned those wrinkles. Those wrinkles mean I've lived a good, hard, and sometimes ugly life. It's through intentionality, tears, reading, conversing, laughing, smiling, frowning and living life full that I've earned my wrinkles.

- I choose today to be okay not being perfect — not having the perfect body, the perfect outfit, the perfect hair or perfect face.

- Today I choose to love every mistake I've made because it's through those mistakes that God gives me an opportunity to grow and be refined.

- I don't have to live in fear. I don't have to feel less than. I am me. Like me or not.

Take that, lies!

xo-Shelley

I believe there is something so powerful that happens when you fall in love with how God made you. When you accept your flaws or the parts of yourself that aren't what you wanted in this life. When you own your uniqueness and your individuality. To me, that is when you are living security well.

Remember that becoming a strong, secure woman is an active process. It is something, I believe, that you always need to be intentional about. Not only by covering the lies in God's truth but also by celebrating and owning your individual uniqueness. Also, remember that awareness and insight are key. Being able to recognize how you feel and/or name what you are experiencing can help you move forward towards health and wholeness. And finally, remember that working through your insecurities is **much less about changing who you are and much more about discovering, embracing and loving yourself.**

CHAPTER TWELVE
Rebuilding Trust

"How will I ever trust my husband again?" "Is this even possible?" "Is it okay to not trust him right now?" " Why does my husband keep telling me to just trust him?" Do any of these questions sound familiar to you? I know for myself, when our process started, I really didn't know that trusting Jason or anybody else would be possible. My hope is working through this chapter, you will get to a place of better understanding what it looks like to rebuild trust in a marriage damaged by sexual betrayal.

I think women desire on an innate level to trust their husband, so when trust is broken, it feels foreign and wrong. In addition, marriage oftentimes feels incomplete when there are trust issues. And it should! It's hard for wives to admit that they don't trust their husbands and sometimes we will try to fabricate a trust that simply isn't present.

I have good news and bad news. The good news is: you are off the hook to be the sole developer of trust in your relationship with your husband. The bad news? You are off the hook to be the sole developer of trust in your relationship with your husband.

I love to be in control. I love to accomplish tasks. Marking a to-do off my list feels oh-so-good. (I've been known to write down tasks I've already completed just so I can feel satisfaction when I draw a line through it!) I also don't like to wait. I don't like to rely on someone else to get things done. And when it comes to the process of rebuilding trust, guess what I get to do: **Wait.** I can't mark "rebuilding trust" off of my to-do list all by myself. And neither can you.

The reason you must wait is because *rebuilding trust is passive for wives and active for husbands.* When I say passive, please understand that this has nothing to do with submission. What I am saying is, wives aren't the ones responsible to rebuild trust when it has been damaged by their husband's sexual betrayal. That's the husband's responsibility. Waiting and releasing this piece of the process to God is not easy. In fact, waiting and playing a passive role when it comes to rebuilding trust is **hard work**. It means you are continually letting go, allowing your husband to figure out how to rebuild trust, allowing your husband to make mistakes along the way, and being clear about your boundaries in the meantime. There are exclusions to most things and this concept of passivity is no different. There are times in this process that wives will have to press into trusting their husbands. I will discuss this at the end of the chapter. But know overall, the onus is on your husband to rebuild trust in the relationship. In addition, this doesn't mean that you sit back and assume that the feelings of trust will someday come. There are still things you can do to help promote the right environment for trust to be restored and below are eight principles to move you towards that end.

Before discussing the eight principles, it's important to consider what it looks like to create the right heart environment for trust to grow. Here's a question you can ask yourself: **What can I do to create the right environment in my heart so that I'm most receptive to my husband's hard work?** Allow this question to sink in. What you want to do is prepare your heart as best you can for the trust to grow, all the while knowing that you play a passive role in the rebuilding of trust.

Also, keep in mind that there is a delicate interplay between waiting and making sure you feel safe throughout this trust rebuilding process. Thus, these principles work towards achieving this balance.

EIGHT PRINCIPLES FOR WIVES (keep in mind that these principles aren't linear in nature but rather synergistic in nature):

Principle #1 - I will give myself permission to not trust my husband.
I mentioned this previously – for you to trust your husband is very natural, innate. So when your trust has been violated, it is especially difficult to allow yourself to sit in a place of distrust. This is an area where you can extend grace and permission to *not* trust your husband until the trust has been restored. When you give yourself permission and grace, you take the burden off, and allow yourself to breathe, watch, wait and see what your husband chooses to do. My friend, Chrissie, said that it was only after she removed the pressure from herself to trust her husband that she was able to move forward in the process. Whoa, that's big.

Principle #2 - I will embrace the fact that forgiveness does not mean I feel trust but rather forgiveness is one component that prepares my heart to trust again.
It seems like wives I talk to often equate forgiveness with trust. Some even equate forgiveness with reconciliation. But at what point did that link become cause-and-effect? The two do not go hand-in-hand. Forgiveness is a choice. It sets you free. It softens your heart. Trust, on the other hand, is a *feeling* and it is also a *state of being*. It is something that is restored with a lot of hard work. Hard work on the wife's part as she prepares the environment of her heart to be receptive to the {hard} work her husband will have to do through *years* of diligence and intentionality.

Principle #3 - I will allow myself to have boundaries in the bedroom.
Think through what you feel comfortable doing (from a sexual stand point) with your husband. Never should a wife feel pressured into doing anything she doesn't want to

do sexually. Nor should she feel like she can save her husband from this addiction by being a person she simply is not in the bedroom.

Jason speaks to this in his book *Worthy of Her Trust* when he says, "the reality is that a wife's sexier behavior may curb his acting out outside the bedroom, but it won't change what happens in his heart and mind inside the bedroom. His character and attitude as it pertains to his sexuality will remain unchanged."[63]

QUESTION #1: Do you feel pressure to behave a certain way in the bedroom? Do you believe that this will stop your husband from acting out?

It is not your fault that your husband chose to act out and betray your marriage. Again, it is not your fault. You cannot control your husband nor prevent him from acting out in the future. By prostituting your body to your husband, you are doing more damage than good in your marriage.

On the other hand, know that there are many wives that say they aren't prostituting their bodies nor are they having sex with their husband to keep him from "acting out". These wives say that in the midst of healing, they enjoy sexual intimacy and the feeling of connection with their husband. Oftentimes, in these situations, sexual intimacy is one of the only forms of intimacy the couple experiences. My hope is that part of your healing journey will be to discover and cultivate other forms of intimacy, which will create a deeper connection with your spouse. We will discuss this further in chapter thirteen.

Principle #4 - I have the right to protect my heart.

You need to feel safe, put up guardrails, and exert some control during the initial stages of the healing process. The length of time you will need to do this will be different for each couple. The timing of when to release your protection is when you, the wife, don't feel you need the guardrail. It's your choice, not your husband's.

Refer to appendix D, starting on page 151 for examples of tools that can be used to set up guardrails as well as to rebuild trust.

QUESTION #2: Which of these strategies in appendix D do you feel you need to implement? What has held you back from implementing the strategies you identified below?

Principle #5 - I will be aware of the fact that triggers have the potential to erode trust.

I mentioned this in chapter four and will discuss it again here because it's that important. When you are triggered, it feels as if you take multiple steps back in your process. Triggers can erode trust and forgiveness. In the after shocks of a trigger, you may feel like you haven't forgiven your husband after all and/or you may believe you cannot and never will trust him. It isn't necessarily that your husband did something to betray your trust, it's that you were triggered. Remember (from chapter four), when you are triggered, a neuro-chemical process occurs and your prefrontal cortex (logic and reasoning) goes off-line. You react.

Keep in mind that when you are triggered (versus an actual breach of trust), you have the opportunity to recognize the truth (this is a trigger, not a breach of trust) and press into not allowing the trigger to completely erode the trust your husband has {hopefully} worked really hard at rebuilding.

QUESTION #3: Can you think of a personal example where a trigger eroded trust in your marriage?

Principle #6 - I will surrender my husband and his process to God
This principle is split into three parts:

- **Recognizing that you can't change your husband but your husband is capable of changing with God's help.** It's imperative that you open your hands wide and let your husband go. Allow God to work in him. He needs to change not only from an integrity standpoint, but just as importantly, there must be a change at the heart level.

- **Recognizing that you can't be your husband's primary motivation to change.** His motivation needs to be first and foremost because God is calling him to live a different life. It also has to be because he realizes his life is out of control and he doesn't want to live this way. After this, he can be motivated by his love for you and the family you've built together. My point is – you want your husband to be motivated by God to change above being motivated by you.

- **Recognizing that you can't be your husband's safety net.** It can be painful to watch those closest to you, primarily your husband, suffer the consequences of his actions. Especially because his actions affect you. It's important that you allow your husband to make mistakes as he works his recovery and not give him a buffer of protection against natural consequences.

By surrendering him to God, as often as you must, you give your husband and thus your marriage the best chance at surviving and thriving.

QUESTION #4: In what areas do you feel you are working over-time to help your husband restore trust in the relationship (typically, an area where your husband should be doing the work)? An example would be reminding your husband of his therapy appointment versus allowing him to remember (or not) his therapy appointment. By your husband remembering the appointment, your husband is rebuilding trust. Likewise, if he doesn't remember his appointment, trust will inevitably decrease.

QUESTION #5: Part of your surrender process, when dealing with principle six, may be to take an emotional step back from your husband (also known as detachment). What does it look like to take a healthy emotional step back from your husband while he works through his process?

Taking an emotional step away from your husband is a bit subjective and it can look different for each wife. Here are a couple of ideas to get you started:

- Living in the present – trying not to focus on the "what if's" of the future or the "if only's" of the past. For instance, "what if my husband doesn't change?" or "what if he chooses his addiction or his mistress over me?" or "If only I had known about his problem sooner."

- Not sharing your deepest thoughts and feelings with your husband as you used to. This is not with the posture of punishing your husband but rather with a posture of protecting yourself.

- Setting boundaries around situations and circumstances that trigger you (revisit chapters four and five on triggers and boundaries, respectively).

- Choosing to stop being your husband's secretary. When you take an emotional step back, you allow the chips to fall where they may. You don't need to remind him of his therapy appointment or his accountability appointment. You step back and watch to see if he is making his recovery the top priority (versus you making his recovery your top priority).

- Review chapter three for a more in-depth discussion on detachment.

Principle #7 - I will work towards Surrendering my Process to God (and wait on His timing)

Often when your husband violates your trust, your struggle with trust permeates into every relationship. Out of self-protection, you trust yourself but not others, thus you can end up holding everyone else at arm's length, including God. You begin to question His timing. *"Why would He allow this?"* *"Why now?"* *"When will God stop the pain?"*

There are many Biblical examples of people trusting themselves more than God and relying on their own timing. The story that comes to mind that illustrates this beautifully is the story of Abraham and Sarah waiting ever so patiently on God to give them a child. Sarah questions God and His promise to her husband as well as His timing. She decides to take matters into her own hands and suggests that Abraham sleep with her maidservant, Hagar (see Genesis chapter 16). Hagar becomes pregnant with Ishmael. Twelve years after Ishmael's birth, God makes good on his promise to Abraham.[64] Sarah becomes pregnant with Isaac and he is born.

There is a whopping twenty-five years between when God made his promise to Abraham and when Isaac was born.[65] I can't even begin to imagine being patient for twenty-five years (much less one) for God to make good on a promise. So I can most definitely relate to the two of them taking matters into their own hands. But the fact remains: Abraham and Sarah didn't trust God nor did they wait patiently. And this caused them and future generations a lot of heartache.

By now you know – I love Kelly Minter. In one of her other books, *No Other Gods*, she says that Ishmael symbolizes doubt, unbelief and fear, while Isaac symbolizes trust, faith and belief.[66] I believe you can use this concept in your life as you are waiting on God to redeem the trust issues in your marriage. It doesn't serve you well to manufacture the restoration of trust by your own will. Think of this as an Ishmael moment. In practical terms, you take matters into your hands by doing things like convincing yourself that you will trust your husband because it's what you *should* do (as in, "I *should* trust him"). Or maybe taking matters into your own hands looks like choosing to walk away from the marriage or choosing to stay in a marriage, all the while God has made it clear that the next step is otherwise.

Instead of creating Ishmael moments when it comes to the rebuilding of trust, I encourage you to wait on God for the Isaac moment. For Him to continue the good work that He has started both in you and in your husband. In practical terms, you don't know exactly what the outcome of your marriage or your trust issues will look like but what you can do is choose to pray to God and fill Him in on the desires of your heart. He cares and He listens. This point is apparent in Genesis chapter 17 when Abraham pleads with God to remember Ishmael and bless him (see Genesis 17:18). And God in turn says "And as for Ishmael, I have heard you: I will surely bless him..." (Genesis 17:20).

QUESTION #6: What component of the trust re-building process do you believe you need to surrender to God (and/or wait on God's timing)?

QUESTION #7: What plea do you have for God? What do you want him to fulfill in your marriage? Do you believe that he hears your cry?

Principle #8 - I will acknowledge that God is trustworthy above all and work towards trusting in Him.

This is very similar to principle seven as there is a close connection between surrender and trust. But I chose to separate these two because I believe that surrendering to God is one step towards fully trusting in God. The Greek word for trust is "batach" in the well-known verse about trusting God with all your heart (Proverbs 3:5). The original meaning of the word meant "to lie helplessly face downwards."[67] I love this imagery of trust; such vulnerability and helplessness. This is your goal – to completely trust in God as you maneuver through this journey.

I see a lot of similarities between my back and forth in trusting God and the vicious cycle the Israelites found themselves in when it came to trusting God. In the Old Testament, the Israelites trust in other gods and then run back to their one true God, trusting in Him. This happened before they left Egypt, while they were wandering for 40 years in the desert, and once they made it to the Promised Land. The same cycle applies to you and me. There are seasons of life where you trust yourself or others more than God and then seasons where you place your trust and hope in the one true God.

Trusting God is a never-ending process. It ebbs and flows, especially when you are hurt so severely by your husband. Learning to trust in God and His plan for your life takes on a whole new meaning. Whether you are in a season where your trust in God is secure or whether you are in a season where your trust is lacking, below are five suggestions you can practice in order to take another step towards Him.

5 suggestions for working towards placing your trust in God:

- **Telling God you want to learn to trust Him.** – It's as simple as that. Pray to God and share with him that you don't trust him and that you'd like to be able to. Then get ready for God to move as he exposes the things in your life that you trust more than Him.

- **Invite others into the process.** – It's important to invite someone else into this part of your process. Tell a trusted friend that you want to learn to trust God. Not only can they be praying for you but also hold you accountable as you take next steps on this journey.

- **Recognizing the idols in your life (as well as what they have to offer) and confessing them to God.** – Kelly Minter, in her study on Nehemiah, says that confession is simply "agreeing with God and telling the truth about a matter."[68] I think it's important for you to recognize what you get from the things in life that you trust more than God. For myself, when I consider the idol of body image or career, I recognize that these things offer me *control, security, power, self-protection* and *identity.*

- **Pressing into God and listening for his voice (through prayer, scripture, a heart of gratitude) to show you the way.** – Think of the times in your life where God has shown up. When has He spoken to you? Start a journal of your "God-Winks".[69] These are the moments when you feel his hand in your every day and know that He is speaking to you.

- **Risk-Taking.** – Jennie Allen says, in her book *Surrender*, "the only exercise that works one-hundred percent of the time to draw one close to the real God is **risk**."[70] This might look like using your voice and stating how you feel. This might look like choosing to focus on gratitude for one day in the midst of feeling like there is nothing to be thankful for.

QUESTION #8: What do you put your trust in *other than God*? (Hint: Think of the ways you have learned to cope and/or what you run to when you are feeling insecure.)

QUESTION #9: Which of the five suggestions do you feel you should practice in your life during this season? Why does the one you picked strike a chord with you?

The reality for me is this: It's in the ugly that I get the **opportunity** to trust God more. It's through my **obedience** that my trust increases. And it's when I **risk/surrender** that God does some of His best work.

As a recap, here is a list of the eight principles:

- **Principle #1** - I will give myself permission to not trust my husband.

- **Principle #2** - I will embrace the fact that forgiveness does not mean I feel trust but rather forgiveness is one component that prepares my heart to trust again.

- **Principle #3** - I will allow myself to have boundaries in the bedroom.

- **Principle #4** - I have the right to protect my heart.

- **Principle #5** - I will be aware of the fact that triggers have the potential to erode trust.

- **Principle #6** - I will surrender my husband and his process to God.

- **Principle #7** - I will work towards Surrendering my Process to God (and wait on His timing).

- **Principle #8** - I will acknowledge that God is trustworthy above all and work towards trusting in Him.

These eight principles help create the right heart environment for trust to grow. Now, I'd like to discuss those moments when you need to *press into* trusting your husband.

I mentioned that pressing into trusting your husband happens when you recognize you are being triggered versus an actual breach of trust (page 102). In my experience, there have been other times as well when I have had to press into trusting Jason. Let me give you an example. When we became pregnant with our first son, Truman, I remember as my belly started to get bigger, my vulnerability started to increase proportionally. I started to worry. Will Jason remain faithful to me? What if he goes back to his old ways? How will I take care of a baby if Jason isn't faithful? The questions didn't go away. When we brought Truman home and the reality started to set in that this baby wasn't going away and I didn't know if I'd ever get to do anything by myself – well, the worry was even greater. I realized that this was an opportunity for me to speak truth to myself. I needed to remind myself of the hard work that Jason had done to rebuild trust with me, and that I had no control over Jason's choices or actions. And last, to remind myself that God is in control and is my ultimate provider.

So when you encounter life seasons or situations where you feel a little more unsafe and insecure, know that these might be times when it's important to press into trusting ultimately God and also your husband, if he has done the crazy hard work to rebuild your trust.

STAYING AFLOAT

I believe that it is critical in the process of trust building (between a husband and wife) to get to a place where you know you will be okay as long as you have God. It's when you place your trust in God that your heart opens up to trust your husband. This is one of the key ingredients in creating the right heart environment for trust to grow. You aren't looking to your husband to be what only God can provide in your life. You must surrender the trust rebuilding in your marriage to Him.

CHAPTER THIRTEEN

Intimacy

I've noticed a lot of times, when people hear the word intimacy, they automatically think I'm talking about sex. There is so much more to intimacy than just sex and that's what this chapter is all about! I've touched on false intimacy (in chapter one) and self-intimacy (in chapter three). Below is a list of some of the different forms of intimacy plus a brief explanation:

- **True Intimacy** – Being fully known, both the good and the ugly. Think of intimacy as in-to-me-see. In a relationship, this would work both ways so being fully known as well as fully knowing another.

- **False Intimacy** – Wearing a mask and not allowing others to fully know you or you them. Keep in mind there is always a shot of the feelings of true intimacy but without the risk of rejection.

- **Self-Intimacy** – Fully knowing you. For example through journaling or by being gut level honest with yourself and understanding your unique and individual preferences, likes and dislikes.

- **Emotional Intimacy** – Fully knowing each other's feelings.

- **Intellectual Intimacy** – Fully knowing each other's thoughts, hopes and dreams.

- **Proximal Intimacy** – Physically being close together (non-sexual), for example sitting in the same room with one another.

- **Recreational Intimacy** – How we have fun together; for example hiking together, playing a card game, walking in the park.

- **Spiritual Intimacy** – Connecting around God, church, the Bible and faith.

- **Non-Sexual Intimacy** – Involves non-sexual touch; an example would be holding hands or hugging a friend.

- **Sexual Intimacy** – Involves touch and is sexual; it's the culmination of intimacy. Reserved specifically for marriage.

QUESTION #1: What words come to mind when you think of true intimacy? How would you feel if someone knew you fully and you knew him or her fully?

When I think of being fully known, both the good and the bad, these are the words that come to mind:

- **Loved**
- **Accepted**
- **Vulnerable**
- **Authentic**
- **Safe**
- **Secure**
- **Cherished**
- **Unique**
- **Full**
- **Comforted**

Feeling these positive emotions and security in the relationship is what I long for. But to get there involves risk. There is an incredible risk of rejection when I allow myself to be fully known. This risk is precisely what sets true intimacy apart from false intimacy. Remember your husband is dealing with an intimacy issue. It is this lack of ability to connect with himself and others that drives the sexual acting out. The risk of being vulnerable and experiencing rejection outweighs the reward of authentic, deeply connected relationships. As discussed in chapter one, things like pornography, strippers, mistresses, and self-gratification come with little to no risk of rejection. Simultaneously they offer a small dose or hit of the positive emotions listed before (e.g. comfort, security, acceptance, love).

Unfortunately, false intimacy comes with a cost to all parties involved. For the men who live this way there is usually a tremendous amount of shame – deep down they don't like who they are. It cost them their sense of self. Often they live with intense anger, criticism, skepticism and a negative, cynical view of the world. It costs them peace, hope and the ability to see the good in life and people.

As you know firsthand, wives also pay a heavy price. This can be in the form of a shattered self-image, through emotional abuse and/or the destruction of any sense of relational security. It costs wives peace, confidence and authentic connection, to name a few.

WORKING TOWARDS TRUE INTIMACY

I appreciate what William Struthers says in his book, *Wired for Intimacy*. He says:

> "Men share with women the same basic needs of humanity. The need for intimacy, to be known and to know, to be close, affirmed, loved; all are human needs. The need for intimacy requires that we understand whom we are and share that with those we long to be known by. As we become more intimate, the other speaks into us things about ourselves that we could not possibly know from the inside. We allow the one we are intimate with to discover us in ways we could not do on our own, and we do so with them. It is a process that develops and deepens over time. We know ourselves more fully because we are known more fully. The intimacy that we have with God and with others enables us to move along the journey toward either sanctification or depravity." [71]

As I read that, I realize just how many years were stolen from both Jason and I as we have coped and hidden behind other things for fear of being fully known. Not only have we hidden from each other but also from our family and from our friends. And here is the thing for me – it's been through the last five plus years in my support group that I've truly learned what it looks like to be intimate with other women. Further, it's been in that confined space that I have taken leaps of faith and admitted some really ugly stuff. Yes, I've risked being rejected but as I reflect on my Go-To Girl's today, they have all remained faithful to me and my journey and me to their journey. It's because of this support group that I've been able to risk with other people in my life - girlfriends, my parents, Jason, even strangers. Friends, this is why support groups are so vital. It's why I believe in groups so much - because they give us the space to be fully known and to know others. It's in this kind of sweet intimacy that God shows up and can do some of his best work.

QUESTION #2: What about you – who comes to mind when you think of someone that fully knows you and you them? Is there anyone on this planet that you share true intimacy with?

If you're having trouble coming up with someone that knows you fully - that's okay. Know that true intimacy is one of the many fruits that can come out of this arduous process.

It's also important to note that when dealing with false intimacy, "we have wired up our brains to mistake intensity for intimacy".[72] Oftentimes I hear wives comment that they don't understand why their husband was doing (fill in the blank with sexual acting out). The wife will go on to say that they felt their relationship was in good shape. Their sex life was great and there really weren't any problems that they saw. If this sounds like your story, then chances are, there was more *intensity* in your relationship than true *intimacy*. In fact, I'd propose that it's nearly impossible to be in relationship with someone with sexual integrity issues and not have issues with true intimacy.

THE ROLE OF SEX IN MARRIAGE

Before we unpack this, I want you to answer the following questions:

QUESTION #3: What is the role of sex in your marriage and why do you have sex?

I'd like to discuss the role of sexual intimacy in marriage for a couple of reasons. First, sex has been misused within the confines of your marriage. This is due to the fact that your husband has used sexual intimacy with you similarly to how he has used sex through pornography, masturbation, mistresses, etc. Second, as you start to heal, you don't want your sexual relationship with your husband in any way to mirror the sexual misuse of the past. It's for these reasons that I want to perhaps give you a different perspective on how to engage sexual intimacy with your husband. Keep in mind, if you aren't married yet or if you are divorced, this is still applicable to you. Who knows what God's plan is for you long-term, so keep reading.

THE BUILDING BLOCKS OF INTIMACY

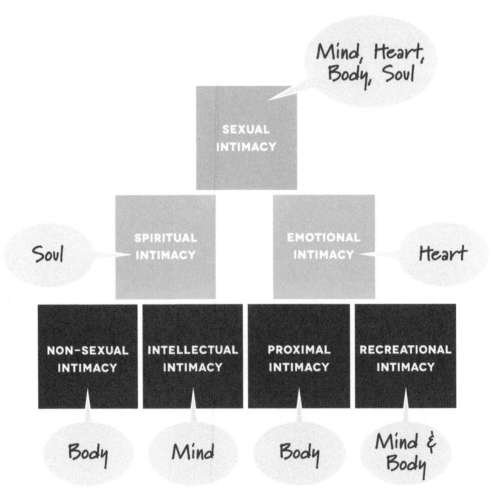

FIGURE 13.1 BUILDING BLOCKS OF INTIMACY

Many people answer the "What is the role of sex and why do you have it" question by saying sex is what they use to connect. Unfortunately, it is often viewed (by both men and women) as a starting point, rather than an end point. When we further look at the role of sexual intimacy in marriage and it's rightful place, it's important to clearly state that **sexual intimacy doesn't start with sex.** It starts with the other forms of intimacy. In my opinion, only after there is a solid foundation of the other forms of intimacy can sexual intimacy be used in a God-honoring way.

Figure 13.1 shows the building blocks of intimacy. You will notice that sexual intimacy is found above the other six types of intimacy, not that it's necessarily the ultimate intimacy but that it's the capstone of the other intimacies. In other words, sexual intimacy shouldn't necessarily be your ultimate goal but rather think of it as a celebration of the other types of intimacies. It's in this way that you can think of the six blocks below sexual intimacy as the core components that lead up to sexual intimacy. As you will notice from the diagram, they all involve one or two of the "core engagers". The four core engagers are heart, mind, body and soul. Another way to think of the core engagers is to think of the part of yourself that you are engaging when you are intimate. So for instance, when you are intimate with your husband in an intellectual way, you are engaging your heart and your mind. When you are intimate with your husband in an emotional way, you are engaging your heart your soul. Sexual intimacy, appropriately so, is the only type of intimacy (when used in a healthy way) that utilizes all of the four core engagers (heart, mind, soul and body).

For myself, engaging on an emotional level (with my heart) and a spiritual level (with my soul) helps propel me towards the truest sexual intimacy with Jason. When Jason and I are not connected on an emotional and/or spiritual level, oftentimes we find that our sexual intimacy is lacking. We try to make it a point to be engaged at a heart and soul level before pursuing sexual intimacy. Oftentimes, this takes a lot of thoughtful, hard work. And it's worth it.

QUESTION #4: If you had to prioritize the building blocks, how would you rank them from most important to least important for yourself?

One of the challenging but helpful things you can do as a couple to facilitate healing is abstain from sex for a period of time. Not only is this abstinence important for your husband's brain to begin to rewire in a healthy way but it also helps other issues surface. I'll talk about the brain rewiring first and then loop back to how abstinence can help in other ways as well.

Remember from chapter one that for your husband, his desire to gratify himself in a sexual way is predicated on his inability to deal with shame and negative emotions. He has learned that when these negative emotions are present he can engage sexually, often to the point of sexual release (orgasm) and subsequently experience a surge of chemicals in his brain. These include dopamine, norepinephrine, epinephrine, adrenaline, oxytocin and serotonin, to name a few. Given this cocktail of chemicals, there are two overriding states that come along with the release. The first is love and the second is euphoria/peace. A function of the chemical release is to bond the person to what he or she just used to gratify himself/herself sexually. When used in the context of true intimacy in marriage, this binds the couple together. When used in an unhealthy way, as your husband has, he becomes bonded to the intensity of the experience. And this begins the unhealthy and destructive neural pathway. For your husband, once he feels triggered by a negative emotion or shame (think the three I's from chapter nine), his brain is on the hunt for the release of chemicals and the resulting sense of love and euphoria. The more he misuses the brain's natural response to sexual stimuli, the more his brain is hard-wired to continue to use and abuse sex. The neural pathway in his brain goes from a two-lane dirt road to an eight-lane superhighway in a short period of time.

You may be wondering – is there any hope then for my husband? And the answer is yes! This is exactly why abstinence is so important. In order to take that neural pathway from a highway to anything less, it needs to stop being used. Over time, this pathway will start to deteriorate. It will never completely go away, but over time it will diminish.

You may be wondering for how long there should be a sexual abstinence within your marriage. One of the pioneers in the sex addiction field, Patrick Carnes, suggests a three to four month period of celibacy in order to promote optimum and healthy sexual intimacy.[73] In terms of neurochemistry, this allows the brain to begin to reboot and begin wiring for healthy sexuality. I have heard of other recommendations for abstinence time frames, so know that there is some variance here.

Remember earlier I said that your husband has learned to mistake intensity for intimacy. A period of abstinence from sexual intimacy, while focusing on developing the other six types of intimacy, can begin to change his neurochemistry. As I've said numerous times, this is yet another area where an experienced counselor or pastor can help.

Sexual abstinence also seems to bring about realizations and other issues to the surface within the marriage that need to be dealt with. For example, some couples report that they realize through the abstinence period that they've forgotten what it looks like to have fun together (recreational intimacy). Others find they've never really known how to connect except through sexual intimacy so this creates an opportunity to learn new ways of connecting. Finally, it's not uncommon to discover some co-dependent tendencies. Specifically, sex has become the way one or both of them make sure the relationship is okay.

No matter what your story is, sex looks different after disclosure than it did before disclosure. When thinking of sexual engagement with your husband (post-disclosure) on a continuum, on one end is the wife that has amped up her sexual intensity with her husband in the hopes of pacifying him. Obviously, deep down, this wife feels a lot of responsibility for the sexual integrity issue. On the other end of the spectrum is the wife that has chosen to protect herself both from a physical standpoint as well as an emotional standpoint. Once she was given a full disclosure, she set a boundary and detached herself both emotionally and physically from her husband.

I was the wife described initially. Today, as I sit here and think through this, I just want to go back and hug that former me and tell her again that this isn't her fault. This isn't her responsibility. And she can't fix it by having more sex with her husband. So please hear it from me: **you don't do your husband or yourself any good when you try to use sex to fix a problem that isn't about sex.**

QUESTION #5: After you found out the ugly truth from your husband, did you set boundaries and choose to hold off on sexual intimacy? Or did you increase the intensity of your sexual intimacy? If you increased it, what did you think it would accomplish?

I want you to give yourself a ton of grace if you increased your sexual intensity post-disclosure. It's a very common, reactive response. Table 13.1 below can help you get back on track.

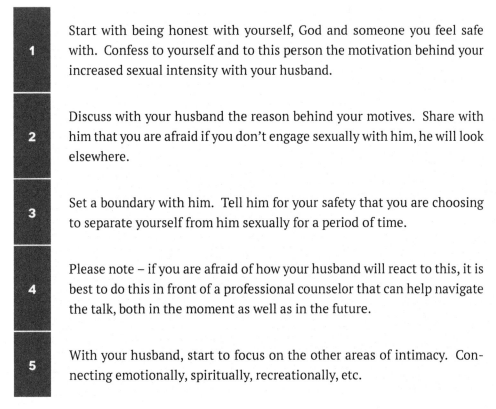

1	Start with being honest with yourself, God and someone you feel safe with. Confess to yourself and to this person the motivation behind your increased sexual intensity with your husband.
2	Discuss with your husband the reason behind your motives. Share with him that you are afraid if you don't engage sexually with him, he will look elsewhere.
3	Set a boundary with him. Tell him for your safety that you are choosing to separate yourself from him sexually for a period of time.
4	Please note – if you are afraid of how your husband will react to this, it is best to do this in front of a professional counselor that can help navigate the talk, both in the moment as well as in the future.
5	With your husband, start to focus on the other areas of intimacy. Connecting emotionally, spiritually, recreationally, etc.

TABLE 13.1 SUGGESTIONS TO HELP SET BOUNDARIES IN THE BEDROOM.

Once you do start to connect again in a sexual way with your husband, know that there will no doubt be a set of triggers you are forced to face. This may look different for each wife, depending on her husband's indiscretions. Here is a sampling of questions you may find yourself asking: *"Whom is he thinking about? Me or Her?" "Did he do this with her, too?" "Is he really desiring me right now or is this all for selfish reasons?"*

Ultimately, sexual intimacy forces you to have continued conversations with your husband. Keep in mind that these difficult conversations are recovery because it's within these conversations that you are being truly intimate. On the other hand, not engaging in these conversations and forcing sexual intimacy without dialogue is the antithesis of recovery. Stop and share with your husband what you are feeling and what you are processing. Even at the expense of it killing the mood. Your thoughts and feelings are more important. Through this part of the process, you are giving yourself permission to grieve your situation at a different level. I will say it again; none of these thoughts or questions should stay in the dark. Drag them into the light so that they aren't as powerful as they feel.

Intimacy is at the heart of this process. It's when you learn to be intimate with yourself, with your husband and with others, that you start to take even greater strides in your journey towards healing and wholeness. Remember that sexual intimacy is the capstone of the other areas of intimacy. In particular, when you are connected to your husband emotionally and spiritually you give yourself the best chance to connect in a God-honoring sexual way. And last, this is an area where you need to give yourself a ton of grace. View this piece of the process as chance for a re-do in the area of sexual intimacy.

CHAPTER FOURTEEN
Why Me?

I never dreamed this chapter would be a part of this workbook. Yet as I started writing about all the big pieces of my process here, I felt like this chapter was necessary. While preparing this material and through conversations with Jason and others, I've considered the following questions: *Why was I attracted to Jason? How could I be attracted to someone with a sexual addiction? What did he do for me in the midst of the dysfunction? Why did our relationship, as dysfunctional as it was, work for me?* I've decided these questions are important for me to answer; I hope you'll decide the same for yourself.

I'm reminded of a conversation I had with one of my good friends, Jennifer, a couple of years into my recovery with Jason. Jen and I met in middle school and we have been good friends since. Jen struggled with a drug addiction in college and for some time after. (You might find it odd that not only my good friend but also my husband was an addict. But as I sit here and type this out, I realize that there was something within me that attracted me to Jen as well.) When this conversation took place, Jen was several years into her sobriety. We were driving in her car and talking about how I was doing and how Jason was doing. She turned to me and she told me that it was important for me to figure out why I was attracted to Jason in the first place. And to figure out what he gave me when he was so sick in his addiction.

Girls, I was so offended. I felt like she was telling me it was my fault - almost as if my pain was inconsequential because I *chose* Jason. As if I could have avoided this. The words hurt. I didn't understand them. I want you to know, she wasn't trying to hurt me and she tried to make that clear. I think I was so fragile at the time that there wasn't much she could say or do. I needed to work through her comments on my own.

That conversation happened ten years ago. It's only been in the last two to three years that I fully understood where she was coming from.

WHY THESE QUESTIONS (AND ANSWERS) ARE SO IMPORTANT

It wasn't until I understood why it was important to answer these questions that I could fully embrace answering them. Here is why I believe the answers to these questions are so important:

- **To fully embrace my brokenness** – By answering these questions, I was able to take a step back and be honest about what I was lacking going into the relationship with Jason. This isn't an indictment on my personhood. Rather, this is a way to be truly humble and honest about my brokenness.

- **To know myself better** – Through this process, I've been given the gift to learn more about myself. These questions allow me to dig deeper into my past and understand myself on a new level.

- **To start to fill those holes in my heart** – It's only after I could see clearly what I was lacking that I could work toward allowing God, myself, and others to start to fill those holes in my heart.

- **To prevent repeating history** – Some of you reading this material will not remain married to your husband. At some point, you might remarry. Some of you have not married yet, but your dating relationships have been with men struggling with these issues. In order to give yourself the best chance of not repeating history, being able to answer these questions is of paramount importance.

IF YOU ARE FEELING DEFENSIVE OR OFFENDED...

Please hear me say: in no way am I implying that you are responsible for your husband's choices. That's not where I'm going with this. What your husband chose to do was painful and irresponsible, and you can't take any responsibility for his actions.

If you are saying to yourself, *"But wait, I didn't know my husband had a sexual integrity issue until after I married him!"* - remember that most of us share this story. Myself included. Understand that there were still underpinnings of the integrity issue before you were privy to your husband's choices. These underpinnings might have been attractive to you or okay with you, even though you had no idea they might one day manifest in your worst nightmare. Read on to understand more about the underpinnings that worked for me in the early days of my relationship with Jason.

HOW I ANSWER THESE QUESTIONS

Part of the reason my relationship worked well with Jason was because we both kept each other at arm's length. He was holding his sexual addiction closest to his heart all the while I was holding my eating disorder closest to mine. We were able to enjoy each other's company but neither of us would allow the other completely in. We both felt wanted and accepted without being fully known. We felt pursued even though there was a façade. The risk of rejection, for both of us, was low. The relationship benefitted us both in this way.

In addition, I came from a family with many rules, black and white, and not a lot of room for error. Jason came from a family where there were little to no rules. He saw things in gray. Jason was refreshing to me. He lived on the edge and this was a respite from the house I grew up in. Being with him gave me a sort of permission to venture into the gray as well.

I couldn't articulate this at the time I met Jason, but as I mentioned in chapter nine, one of my core wounds was feeling unchosen. I felt chosen by Jason, which was something I hadn't felt before from another boy (we were 18 when we met, so boy seems more appropriate than man). This was huge. In effect, Jason filled that gaping hole in my heart.

And last, I thought Jason thought I was perfect. Obviously I wasn't. But I wanted to be. I think part of his shame told him I was perfect. He has said he was drawn to my sexual naïveté, primarily as an offset to his sexual promiscuity. And I allowed this perfection façade to continue for years.

BE BRAVE

So I'm asking you to take a breath and be brave with me. Here are the questions I'd like for you to consider:

QUESTION #1: Why were you attracted to a man with a sexual integrity issue/sexual addiction? What did he do for you? Why did the relationship, as dysfunctional as it was, work for you? What did the relationship give you?

Answering these questions becomes even more important if being in relationship with men with a sexual addiction/integrity issue is a theme in your life. Only by answering the "why" behind your choices can you work towards making better choices in the future.

STAYING AFLOAT

Being able to verbalize why you were attracted to your husband and why the relationship worked can help give you continued insight into yourself. It helps you to see your past clearly. And in that way, it can influence your future. Put another way, "the past is your ally in repairing your present and ensuring a better future."[74]

CHAPTER FIFTEEN
Being Better Because of it All

So you've made it to the final chapter! You've come a long way with me! I'm glad you've stuck it out. My hope is you've learned a lot about yourself through this material and the people you're sharing this journey with. Hopefully you are keeping your head above water or better yet, hopefully you've got your life preserver or better still climbed aboard the rescue boat. And maybe, just maybe, you are beginning to see glimmers of redemption along this arduous and exhausting process.

You and me and a lot of other women all hold something in common. We were personally affected by our husband's sexual betrayal. Sure, our stories all look a little different and take on a life of their own. But we each share a little bit of this common fabric in our hearts and in our souls. I don't think either of us ever saw this coming, did we? I know I never ever thought this would be my story. But it is. And it's also yours. And what I didn't know as I tried to start picking up the pieces was that in the end – I'd be a better, new, different person because of it all. You see, it was just the thing that I needed in my life to wake me up, to get my attention, to realize I needed a rescue. You may be thinking: *"I didn't need this in my life to get my attention. I was awake, thank you."* And this very well may be the case. But I DO believe wholeheartedly that we each have a decision to make:

> Will we allow what has happened in our lives to foster a heart of bitterness, distrust and coldness? Or will we allow our story to serve as an opportunity to grow in character, strength and truth?

Know that through this experience and through this process, you *can* become an even better you. This situation doesn't have to be something that will pull you down forever. You are worth being rescued. That's the truth.

As we look at Scripture, God promises us that our trials and temptations aren't for not. In James 1:2, James urges us to "consider it pure joy" when we encounter various trials because it is through these trials that our faith is tested which produces perseverance. He goes on to urge us to allow perseverance to "finish its work" so that we may be "mature and complete, not lacking anything." Know that it is through our trials that God tests us. And it is through our trials that if we are willing, God will develop our character. And it is through our trials that we become better and God is glorified.

QUESTION #1: Do you believe that God will use this part of your story and this season in the desert to ultimately bring glory to Him and to refine you and sculpt you into a new creation?

I want you to know that it's okay if you don't believe this in your heart and in your mind. Or it may be that you know it in your mind but in the depths of your heart and soul, you just don't feel it yet.

I can tell you, it's taken me a long time to get to this place of knowing for certain that I am a better person because of what Jason and I have been through. As I look back, I didn't want to admit that for a long time. So God made it clear as day to me. It's a story I love to share and want to close with it here:

About two and a half years ago now, Jason and I were in California where Jason was speaking at a men's retreat at a church. He had left early the morning of and I was to meet him at the church later and had agreed to share a bit from my perspective with the guys in attendance. I headed out for a run and I remember asking God what exactly He wanted me to share with the men that afternoon. And what I heard Him say was: *"It was for your good."* I remember wanting to swat the words away. I may have even laughed. And I may have rolled my eyes. Maybe. But deep down, I knew it was truth. Once back at the hotel, I headed to my room where my Bible awaited me. I knew those words sounded familiar. And I came across two verses. Romans 8:28 says "And we know that in all things God works together for the good of those who love him, who are called according to his purpose." The other was towards the end of Genesis. It was the story of Joseph. If you haven't read this story in its entirety, I want you to do so. It's a beautiful story of forgiveness. Joseph was betrayed deeply by his brothers. He not only spent time in a well he also spent time in prison all starting with his brother's betrayal. God continued to test Joseph for a total of thirteen years before He allowed him to sit on the throne of Egypt.[75] Wow, the trust and faith Joseph displayed is amazing. Towards the end of Genesis, Joseph's brothers are reunited with him. They fall to his feet in fear. And Joseph tells them: "You intended to harm me, but God intended it for good..." (Genesis 50:20). The word "good" originates from the Hebrew word "towb". The word "towb" literally means "good in the widest sense" or "good in every sense of that word".[76] A couple of synonyms for "good" are "pleasing" and "welcome".[77] As I sit back and let these words sink in, I am here to tell you that it was through Jason's sexual addiction coming to light and through our recovery that God has done some of his best work in me. It was for my good. And I mean that in the widest sense. If I could go back in time, I wouldn't have it any other way.

COUNTING BLESSINGS

Let me share with you some of the blessings that God has graciously given me:

- First and foremost, the greatest gift God has given me is a redeemed marriage. God rescued both Jason and I and continues to do so as we find our way both individually and as a couple. Jason and I have three beautiful little boys, each with a different color of hair and a unique personality. They're the children that I wasn't sure would ever come to fruition when we started this process. God has given me a bevy of beautiful women to support through phone and in-person groups. They are a treasure to me. I have my Go-To Girls that love me and encourage me in my journey. We have been committed to each other for years now and still meet every other week to encourage and push each other on our individual journeys.

- I have worked hard at coming to terms with some of the poor choices I have made in the past surrounding my eating disorder, including making amends with people I hurt some seventeen years ago.

- I experience a love and admiration for my husband that I never thought would be possible. I respect him more than anyone on the planet. My respect for him is even wider given where he was and how far he has come. I've been given a front-row seat in watching the love of my life change in incredible ways. I could go on but I will stop there.

QUESTION #2: Will you stop now and take some time to think through what life might look like for you five or ten years down the road? What blessings do you believe might come out of this trial? What blessings do you already see? What do you hope to gain through all of this?

I never want my pain to be in vain. God is a God of using our deepest hurts to not only glorify Him but to also serve and encourage others in their process. 2 Corinthians 1: 3-4 speaks to this very thing: "Praise be to the God and Father of our Lord Jesus Christ who comforts us in all our troubles, so that we can comfort those in any trouble with the comfort we ourselves receive from God." My hope for each of you is that at some point, you grab a life preserver and become a part of the rescue crew.

Your final exercise in this workbook is to go back to that woman within yourself that was barely keeping her head above water. Think back to those first days and weeks, to those hours after realizing that your marriage and life weren't what you thought they were. **What do you wish you could have told yourself? What advice would you give yourself?** Take time to think through what you'd like for this woman (I mean you) to know. Here is a sample letter just to get your mind thinking.

Dear Me,

You were so young when this all started – just 26 years. You were so innocent. You thought he only had eyes for you. Little did you know that he was sick. Very sick. And so were you. You just didn't realize it yet.

When you started wondering if he was lying about his whereabouts — don't deny that inner voice telling you there was something terribly wrong. Because there was. And that voice of truth was worth keeping around. Little did you know, it would take years to find that voice again. When you asked him over and over why you didn't feel connected to him, don't believe the lies in your head: "I'm just crazy. I ask for too much. I need to have more sex with him."

When you decided enough was enough and you were ready to work on that garden of bitter weeds in your heart — know that that decision was one of the best decisions you ever made.

Don't feel too bad about calling the other woman. It was out of that conversation that you knew there was a serious problem.

When you planned your confrontation and your heart was beating wildly. As Astro comforted you while you waited for him to get home from his business trip, know that you were doing exactly what you needed to do.

As you started to process the disclosure — I want you to know that it wasn't your fault, you weren't responsible. It wasn't because you didn't have enough sex with him. You didn't need to forgive him right away or try to change who you were in order to save your marriage. And when that first counselor asked you what your responsibility was in all of this, don't believe a word he says. He doesn't know what he's talking about and besides, God had an incredible counselor lined up for you guys.

You did some amazing work those first three years. You forgave him. You chose to stay. Little did you know but those decisions would also be some of the best you have ever made. Even though there were days when you wondered if you truly had forgiven him and even though there were days when you wondered if you'd made the right choice to stay married to him — it's okay. It was the right choice and forgiveness, well, forgiveness is a journey in and of itself.

When you decided to take a break from your recovery and found yourself three years later still on that break — know that God doesn't waste anything in this life. It's out of that long break as your heart turned cold and dead that ultimately awakened you to the life you were created to live.

When you delivered your first baby boy with him at your side, it's okay that you were scared of the future. Little did you know that over the next five years, you'd give birth to two more baby boys. The babies you thought you might not have with the man of your dreams.

And it was such a good thing that you saw him pave the way taking small steps every day towards wholeness and health. It was he that inspired you to start to work on your stuff.

And when you started to really work on your stuff — know that it was worth it. As hard as the dark places are, know that there is light in the morning...

Love,
me

Now it's your turn. Take some time to write a letter to yourself beginning back at the time you had those inklings something was terribly wrong in your marriage. May this letter help you see how far you've come. (Let me also say, if you don't feel you are ready to write such a letter to yourself, that's okay. Skip this exercise and come back to it at a later date when you feel more ready.)

Dear Me,

APPENDIX A
Getting Ready for the First Session

Hello! Welcome! Let me just tell you, we are so excited to work with you as you take your next step towards healing and wholeness. Please know that we have been praying for you and for God to work in amazing ways as we move forward as a group. Below are a couple of things to keep in mind as we start the group together.

- **Safety:** Our job is to make sure that this group is safe for each of you. This is where you are allowed to come as you are. Put on your comfy pants. Grab a cup of hot tea. And please, be you. Take total advantage. Bring whatever it is that you are afraid to share. This is the place to do it. Together, we will work hard towards being real, honest, and vulnerable.

- **Respect:** What is shared within the group, stays within the group. We will not judge others or ourselves. We will work through our shame and embarrassment. We will support each other and encourage each other. We are each in a different place in our individual journeys and that is all right. We will actively listen to the other women and give them feedback, as needed.

- **Community:** One of the best things about this group is the opportunity to build community. This is a group of women that have agreed to journey together during this season. Be intentional. Try to connect with each other outside of group. Groups that thrive are groups that spend some amount of time connecting outside of the time spent on the conference call.

- **Focus on Self:** You are welcome to come to group to vent about your relationship. This is the place to do it. And we also know that we can't change anybody but ourselves. So we will look towards empowering ourselves and loving ourselves throughout this process.

- **My Why:** We will think through why we have decided to be a part of this support group. What do you hope to accomplish through our time together? Think through what your goals are and record them on page 146.

- **The One Thing:** After each session, you will ask yourself: what is the one thing I've taken away from our time together. It may be a light bulb moment that you experienced. It may be the words from someone else's mouth that spoke to you in a profound way.

- **Saying Good-Bye:** You might feel like you've signed up for a lifetime of group when you committed to six months! Know that it goes quickly. Whether you choose to continue after that or not is certainly up to you. When you are starting to feel like it's time to say good-bye, reach out to your facilitator to discuss this further. Also, be aware that we want to take time, as a group, to say good-bye to you and to process your departure.

THE ESSENTIALS

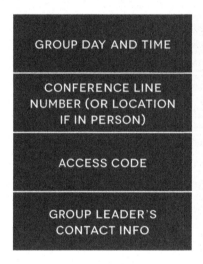

GROUP DAY AND TIME

CONFERENCE LINE
NUMBER (OR LOCATION
IF IN PERSON)

ACCESS CODE

GROUP LEADER'S
CONTACT INFO

GROUP MEMBERS CONTACT INFO

Below are a couple of things to keep in mind for your group phone conferences.

- If possible, try to be in a **quiet place away from distractions**. We are all busy and I know this can't always be the case. But if possible, try to focus completely on the call so that you get the most out of it (this means no checking email, texting, surfing the internet, etc.).

- There are absolutely times when you may be driving or handing off children when the call starts. Please go ahead and dial in, let us know you are on the call, and then **mute your phone (*6 from your key pad if you don't have a mute feature on the phone itself)** until you are in a quiet place. Also, please give me the heads up if you need to share at a particular time of the call (if you will be in a transition at some point during the call).

- Although I try not to interrupt, know that I may need to under the following circumstances:
  - o   If I am having trouble hearing you
  - o   If there is a lot of back ground noise
  - o   If we are running out of time and we need to move on
  - o   If I sense the group may need clarification

- If you are **dropped from the call** or having any technical issues, please contact your facilitator via text. We will see your text come through and will do what we can to help resolve the issue.

CHECK-IN FAQ'S

- **What is a check-in?** Checking in is simply what we call the time we spend discussing and processing the hard stuff from the last two weeks. Initially, it may help to look at the sample questions (on the next page) and as you get more accustomed to digging deep and talking about things below the surface, you won't need to use the questions. This isn't the time to talk about your aunt's cousin's sister-in-law. Or the weather. This is the time to talk about you. And what you have been struggling with. What you have worked through. What you need feedback on.

- **Sample Questions:** (Use the questions below as a guide)
  - How did I do expressing myself this week?
  - High moment (happiness, joy) of the week?
  - Current emotion (refer to feelings wheel)?
  - Where am I with God (in regards to your situation)?
  - What am I working on?
  - Where am I at in the process?
  - What have I learned about myself this week?
  - Where am I at with self-image?
  - What did God teach me this week?
  - How did I do taking care of myself this week?
  - What made me laugh this week?

- **About how long can I share?** The exact amount of time to share depends on how many women are on the call. Plan to share for about ten minutes and then there should be about four to five minutes after this for feedback. The call goes quickly, so *before you get on the call every two weeks, think through the most important couple of things you'd like to share* and what you'd like to have feedback on. Although we try not to interrupt, know that your facilitator will be watching the clock and may need to interrupt and move the group on if we are pressed for time. Thanks in advance for understanding.

- **I feel nervous about sharing. What do I do?** Please know that if you feel nervous, it's totally normal. We all get nervous! Take a deep breath and remember that we are not here to judge each other but rather to support each other. Come as you are. Nerves and all. I promise, after a couple of sessions, you won't be near as nervous and before long, you will feel right at home.

- **What exactly does it mean to give feedback?** As mentioned above, after someone shares, it's important to give feedback. The way I think of it is like this: when a wife shares, it's as if she has put her heart on the table. Raw, vulnerable, and exposed. By giving her feedback, you are helping her put her heart back in her chest. Giving feedback starts with actively listening. It's also looking for positive points in what the speaker shares. It's about validating her feelings and possibly offering a suggestion. It's about acknowledging her pain and also stating how you can relate to what she is experiencing. And last, feedback is answering this question: *"What does the speaker need based on what she shared?"* [78]

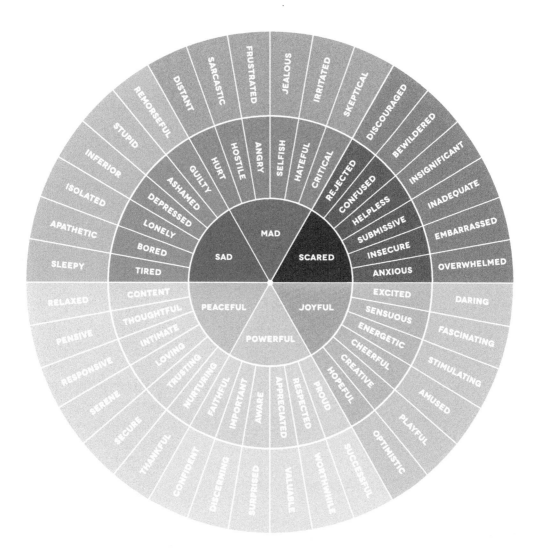

Here's how to use the feeling wheel: typically when we feel an emotion, we can identify it as one of the six primary emotions found on the inside of the circle (sad, mad,
scared, joyful, powerful and peaceful). As we focus on our feelings throughout this
process, this wheel can help us identify more specifically what we are feeling underneath one of the primary emotions. Thus, we are able to talk more clearly about our
emotions and make connections that we otherwise may not have been able to make.
Keep it handy during the week and during group. The feeling wheel was developed by
Dr. Gloria Willcox. Used by permission.

One of the first things we will do as a group is we will share our stories with each other. This can be very difficult, especially if you haven't shared your story with anyone.

There are two main reasons that we share our stories within this group. First, and most obviously, it's the best way for each of us to get to know each other and understand completely where the other is coming from. Second, when we share our story, we are intentionally choosing to integrate our stories into our psyches and accepting what God has allowed in our lives. In essence, we are accepting the reality of our lives. Third, we are practicing intimacy. We'll unpack this and explain it more in a couple different sections of the workbook. Finally, I also find that as I share my story, I begin to make connections and have light bulb moments that I otherwise wouldn't have had if I hadn't talked out loud about the wounds from my past. I believe that God can use our stories, when we speak them out loud, not only to heal us but to also minister to others.

TRAUMA

Sharing our stories does have the potential to trigger trauma from the past (both for the sharer as well as for those listening). If you start to feel overly anxious or upset, please let your facilitator know so that together we can decide what you can do to move forward. It's helpful for me, as someone else is sharing, to remember that it's not my story. My story is my story and your story is your story. We don't have to take on each other's stories. We are each on a unique journey and although there are similarities woven into each of our stories, there are also a lot of differences.

THINK IT THROUGH

Before we meet for the first time, please take some time to think through the highs and lows of your story. Think back to your childhood. What events shaped you into who you are today? What were your struggles? It's also important to think through what life was like when you met your husband (or boyfriend or x-husband, depending on your specific situation.) Also, it's important to discuss what transpired both before and after you realized your significant other has a problem with sexual integrity. Last, think through what life has been like for you since your world forever changed. It may be helpful to take some notes of the major talking points you'd like to mention. Plan on sharing for about twenty minutes. This is enough time to understand where each of us is coming from but certainly isn't enough time for us to go through every detail. You may use the next page to take some notes of what you'd like to share with the group.

My Story

My Story

Use the space below to take notes about each group member as they share their story. Once we have all shared, the stories start to run together so it's nice to jot down the things you feel are relevant about each person.

Take some time to think through what you'd like to work on over the next six to twelve months. Come up with at least two goals. Rather than look at the end result of this whole journey, try to set your goals as a next step on the journey. But remember, anything goes here. Just keep in mind that these are personal goals. Think through what you'd like to change and what you'd like to see an improvement on specifically within yourself yet related to your healing process in regards to sexual betrayal.

APPENDIX B
Healthy Self-Care Strategies

- Healthy self-talk- this means no "I should have's" or negative talk.
- Getting it out – journaling or talking to a trusted friend.
- Exercise.
- A warm bath.
- Snuggling on the couch with your little/s.
- Sitting by the fire and reading a good book.
- Listening to your favorite music.
- Heading to bed early and journaling or reading.
- A walk in nature.
- Prayer.
- Organizing.
- Hobbies like photography, knitting, gardening, and painting.
- Worship nights at church.
- Coffee or another favorite drink.
- Taking a different route to and from work in order to avoid a certain location (whether it be a billboard or otherwise) that reminds you of your husband's past.
- Grocery shopping and running errands sans husband.
- Night away at a hotel.
- Women's retreat.
- Ordering in or eating out.
- Hiring a housekeeper occasionally or permanently.
- Brunch with a girlfriend.
- Ten minutes of stillness.
- Sunshine.

APPENDIX C

Trigger Five Step Process

(Go to rlforwomen.com/resources for an electronic copy of this handout.)

STEP ONE: IDENTIFY PAST OR POTENTIAL TRIGGER

STEP TWO: IDENTIFY HOW THIS TRIGGER MAKES ME FEEL AND WHY

STEP THREE: IDENTIFY WHAT I NEED IN ORDER TO FEEL SAFE

STEP FOUR: IDENTIFY WHAT ASSISTANCE MY HUSBAND CAN GIVE (NONE, START OR STOP) AND FOR THOSE APPLICABLE TO MY HUSBAND, REQUEST MY NEED

STEP FIVE: ALLOW GOD'S TRUTH TO SPEAK INTO THE TRIGGER

INTERNET FILTERING AND MONITORING (I.E. CONVENANT EYES, SAFE EYES, ETC.)

Internet *filtering* will allow one to filter the content allowed on specific computers or smart phones. Internet *monitoring* records the activity on the electronic device. Internet monitoring and filtering "is more of a speed bump versus a road-block".[79] The reality is, most men that are ensnared in a sexual integrity issue are creative and Internet savvy. They know loopholes around these monitoring devices. For instance, recently I heard of a man that changed the language of his phone to German. Once he did this, he had free reign to access any of the sites he wanted to without the Internet monitoring device flagging his activity. For more information on both internet filters and monitors, visit: www.redemptiveliving.com/resources

GPS PHONE TRACKING

It's easy to install an app on any smart phone to track the phones whereabouts via GPS coordinates. Although this can be a potential way to rebuild trust, there are professionals, like Jason, that don't believe they are your best bet. One will find that the exact location of the phone is give or take fifty feet. This can make a huge difference when it comes to rebuilding trust. So, if you so choose to use GPS phone tracking, pair it with another strategy in order to be able to cross-check your husband's whereabouts.

STD TESTING

STD testing is never something I like to discuss. But the reality is, we must protect ourselves on every level. Especially from an unwanted STD. I do not waver when it comes to STD testing. If I talk to a wife that isn't sure exactly what her husband has done but she believes he has been unfaithful to her in *any* way, I recommend that she get tested. Furthermore, if your husband has given you full disclosure and says he had physical contact with another person, you should get tested. Until you obtain the results of the testing, I recommend you abstain from any sexual contact with your husband.

IN-HOUSE OR OUT-OF-HOUSE SEPARATION

A separation is often implemented either at the beginning of the process when a wife first discovers her husband has been living a double life or during the early stages of the process if her husband consistently breaks boundaries. The separation should never be used as punishment towards your husband but rather as a means for protecting yourself from further damage. It may be necessary to reframe your view of a separation. **Think of a separation as a step towards healing and reconciliation rather than a step towards divorce.** If you need time to process and sort through the facts as well as your feelings, a separation may be a good idea. If your husband is continuing to break the boundaries that the two of you have agreed upon, then a separation may be a good idea. If your husband is working hard on restoring the relationship but you'd like to see him suffer a little more, then a separation probably isn't the best option for you.

T-30 JOURNAL

This is a journal that Jason initially used to help rebuild trust with me in the beginning stages of our healing. Every day, he would log where he was and what he was doing in the back of his planner. The beauty of this isn't so much found in the fact that I would know his whereabouts when we reviewed it at the end of the day; but rather the intention and heart behind the journal. The fact that Jason was willing to diligently keep track of his experiences every thirty minutes, day in and day out, helped slowly plant the seeds of trust. This was huge for me because up until this point in our relationship, Jason's whereabouts had always seemed vague to me. I was always left wondering what he had really been doing with his time. In addition, reviewing the information with him in the evening showed me that he truly cared about rebuilding the trust in our relationship. Even if it meant he had to write down his whereabouts in thirty-minute increments.

Early on in our recovery, we took time every evening to process our emotions from the day. We were fortunate in that we didn't have children yet so our evenings were our evenings. But even if you do have children, a daily check-in is critical. I find that most wives that I talk to put a lot of weight in the daily check-ins. To a certain extent, they are able to gauge how committed their husbands are to the process by if they have been checking-in (or not). Jason uses a familiar counseling tool called a FAN (Feeling – Affirmation – Need) in his office. He has tweaked the FAN a bit and also tailors the FAN to the couple's specific needs. For instance, I've heard a wife say that her husband did or did not do a FANIT. (My husband is very creative.) Just to give you a flavor of what this looks like, below is what the FANIT stands for. (Remember, this is a tool for your husband to use to start to rebuild trust and emotional intimacy). The husband goes through the following checklist:

> **Feeling:** What am I feeling now and why. And a time in my childhood between the ages of 6-16 when I felt that.
> **Affirmation:** Affirming something in your wife, the more focused on character, the better.
> **Need:** Asking your wife what she needs.
> **Integrity:** This is both what I have done and what I have not done. It is a check in regarding any acting out activity, as well as the thoughts and behaviors that prevent returning to those activites.
> **Triggers:** Are there any triggers that you, as a wife, would like to share with me?

If you choose to use this tool, think about how you can tailor it to your specific needs.

A couple of days ago I was visiting with a wife over coffee. She was asking me about these daily check-ins. I initially told her that Jason and I don't do check-ins anymore. But the more I sat there thinking it through, I realized that check-ins have integrated into the fabric of our lives. No, we don't sit down every evening and do a formal check-in but we do connect most evenings and discuss our deeper feelings, needs and wants. It's a beautiful way to live and it started with the daily check-ins.

ACCOUNTABILITY PARTNER

I highly recommend the use of this tool for couples. Not only for husbands but also for wives. For husbands, they should find a person (and preferably three people) that will be willing to meet with them every week. Jason dedicates an entire chapter to this in his book *Worthy of Her Trust*, so I'm not going to go into detail here about the dynamics of an accountability group for men. However, I do want to mention that it can be helpful when the men your husband has chosen to meet with are men that you find honorable and filled with integrity. If your husband wants to meet with a friend that you know lacks integrity, you get the right to request they stop meeting. If your husband is at a loss for finding guys that can hold him accountable (which is very common), many local churches host accountability type groups, so that may be the best place to start. For wives, it is also helpful to have a small group of women that will love you and support you as you walk through this process.

WEEKLY COUNSELING

It's a given that counseling can help you navigate the ins and outs of this process. The counselor can also help you figure out how to set appropriate and healthy boundaries to keep your heart safe. Early on, I didn't know if Jason was willing to do what it took to change his ways. But what I did see was that he was committed to counseling. Find a counselor that specializes in sexual integrity issues. Keep searching until you find the right fit. We agreed early on that counseling was Jason's responsibility. He would make the appointments, remind me the day of, etc. And if we had children, I would have expected him to find childcare. Allowing your husband to lead in this area is an excellent way for him to begin rebuilding trust. It's a huge responsibility. In my opinion, women that have to pull their husbands to counseling should spend their money and time elsewhere.

FIVE MINUTE RULE

If I had to have a favorite tool that helped me feel safe, this one was it. Our counselor, Bryan implemented this early on in our process. We (Jason, Bryan and I) collectively agreed that if I ever called Jason, he would have five minutes to return my phone call. If he didn't return my call within the allotted time, I would assume the worst of his whereabouts. I can't even begin to tell you how much peace of mind this gave me during those early months. I highly recommend it.

24-HOUR DISCLOSURE RULE

If you, as a wife, want to know when your husband has broken a sexual integrity boundary, then a twenty-four hour disclosure rule will help keep your anxiety at bay. What you and your husband are agreeing to, is that if he were to act out in any way, he has twenty-four hours to come to you, confess what he has done, make amends, etc. Not only will this help us wives feel safer; but with this agreement, we also don't have to waste our time playing detective. It also benefits the husband in that it provides "another layer of accountability" and an "added motivation towards integrity."[80]

FINANCIAL ACCOUNTABILITY

I believe Jason says it best when he says that in the process of rebuilding trust, there is a lot of ambiguity and subjectivity. But when it comes to spending money, it doesn't get more objective and tangible.[81] Thus, this is an area where men can capitalize on rebuilding trust. For us wives, consider what you need in this area in order to feel safe. For instance, if your husband discloses that he kept a secret bank account that you weren't aware of or if you find out that he spent thousands of dollars at a strip club, this is an area where you should think through what you need in order to feel safe. I know a couple that sat down every week and did a financial review with each other. Not only was this a strategy the wife used to feel safer (from a financial perspective); it was also how they monitored a goal that they had agreed to. The agreement being for him to slowly replenish the savings that he had spent on his addiction.

APPENDIX E
Session Notes

SESSION #1	
DATE	
WHAT I'D LIKE TO SHARE	
NOTES	
QUESTIONS	
THE ONE THING	

DATE

WHAT I'D LIKE
TO SHARE

NOTES

QUESTIONS

THE ONE
THING

DATE

WHAT I'D LIKE
TO SHARE

NOTES

QUESTIONS

THE ONE
THING

DATE

WHAT I'D LIKE
TO SHARE

NOTES

QUESTIONS

THE ONE
THING

DATE

WHAT I'D LIKE
TO SHARE

NOTES

QUESTIONS

THE ONE
THING

DATE

WHAT I'D LIKE
TO SHARE

NOTES

QUESTIONS

THE ONE
THING

DATE

**WHAT I'D LIKE
TO SHARE**

NOTES

QUESTIONS

**THE ONE
THING**

DATE

WHAT I'D LIKE
TO SHARE

NOTES

QUESTIONS

THE ONE
THING

DATE

WHAT I'D LIKE
TO SHARE

NOTES

QUESTIONS

THE ONE
THING

DATE

WHAT I'D LIKE
TO SHARE

NOTES

QUESTIONS

THE ONE
THING

DATE

WHAT I'D LIKE TO SHARE

NOTES

QUESTIONS

THE ONE THING

DATE

WHAT I'D LIKE
TO SHARE

NOTES

QUESTIONS

THE ONE
THING

DATE

WHAT I'D LIKE
TO SHARE

NOTES

QUESTIONS

THE ONE
THING

DATE

WHAT I'D LIKE
TO SHARE

NOTES

QUESTIONS

THE ONE
THING

DATE

WHAT I'D LIKE TO SHARE

NOTES

QUESTIONS

THE ONE THING

DATE

WHAT I'D LIKE
TO SHARE

NOTES

QUESTIONS

THE ONE
THING

DATE

WHAT I'D LIKE
TO SHARE

NOTES

QUESTIONS

THE ONE
THING

DATE

WHAT I'D LIKE
TO SHARE

NOTES

QUESTIONS

THE ONE
THING

DATE

WHAT I'D LIKE
TO SHARE

NOTES

QUESTIONS

THE ONE
THING

DATE

WHAT I'D LIKE
TO SHARE

NOTES

QUESTIONS

THE ONE
THING

NOTES

CHAPTER 1:   1   Patrick Carnes, *Out of the Shadows* (Center City, MN: Hazelden, 3rd Ed, 2001), 26.

2   Ibid., 99-101.

3   Ibid., 99.

4   Ibid., 99-102.

5   Pornography Statistics. (n.d.). Retrieved March 19, 2015, from http://www.provenmen.org/2014pornsurvey/pornuseatwork/

6   Pornography Statistics. (n.d.). Retrieved March 19, 2015, from http://fightthenewdrug.org/the-problem-with-porn/#sthash.xlXwSJtN.dpbs

7   William M Struthers, *Wired for Intimacy*, (Downers Grove, IL: Intervarsity Press, 2009), 20.

CHAPTER 2:   8   Barbara Steffens and Marsha Means, *Your Sexually Addicted Spouse: How Partners Can Cope and Heal* (Far Hills, NJ: New Horizon Press, 2009), 26.

9   Ibid., 62.

10   Melody Beattie, *Codependent No More: How to Stop Controlling Others and Start Caring for Yourself* (Center City, MN: Hazelden, 1992), 33.

11   Patrick Carnes, *Out of the Shadows* (Center City, MN: Hazelden, 3rd Ed., 2001), 128.

12   Melody Beattie, *Codependent No More*, 33.

13   Barbara Steffens and Marsha Means, *Your Sexually Addicted Spouse*, 23-24.

14   Patrick Carnes, *Out of the Shadows*, 113.

15   Ibid., 133-138.

16   Barbara Steffens and Marsha Means, *Your Sexually Addicted Spouse*, 98.

CHAPTER 3:   17   Laurel Mellin, Wired for Joy: *A Revolutionary Method for Creating Happiness from Within* (Carlsbad, CA: Hay House, 2010), 97.

18   Barbara Steffens and Marsha Means, *Your Sexually Addicted Spouse* (Far Hills, NJ: New Horizon Press, 2009), 221.

19   Thank you Tammy S for explaining this to our group one evening. I love this word picture and it's proved helpful to other wives as well!

CHAPTER 4:   20   Amy Arnsten, "Stress signaling pathways that impair prefrontal cortex structure and functioning, "*Nature Reviews Neuroscience* 10, no.6 (2009): 410-422.

21   William Struthers, *Wired for Intimacy* (Downers Grove, IL: Intervarsity Press, 2009), 93.

22   Ibid., 93.

23   Arnsten, "Stress signaling pathways that impair prefrontal cortex structure and functioning, 410-422.

24   Ibid., 410.

25   Ibid., 410-422.

26   Ibid., 410-422.

27   Ibid., 410-422.

28   Marsha Means, *Journey to Healing and Joy* (A Circle of Joy Press, 2011), 94-101.

29   Barbara Steffens and Marsha Means, *Your Sexually Addicted Spouse* (Far Hills, NJ: New Horizon Press, 2009), 126-136.

30   Marsha Means, *Journey to Healing and Joy*, 96.

CHAPTER 5:   31   Henry Cloud and John Townsend, *Boundaries: When to Say Yes, When to Say No, To Take Control of Your Life* (Grand Rapids, MI: Zondervan, 1992), 52.

32   Ibid., 64.

33   Debra Laaser, *Shattered Vows: Hope and Healing for Women Who Have Been Sexually Betrayed* (Grand Rapids, MI: Zondervan, 2008), 48.

CHAPTER 6:   34   Melody Beattie, *Co-Dependent No More* (Center City, MN: Hazelden, 1992), 136.

35   Ibid., 136.

CHAPTER 7:   36   Gary Chapman, *The Other Side of Love* (Wheaton, IL: Tyndale House Publishers, 1999), 21.

37   Ibid., 25.

38   Ibid., 18.

39   Henry Cloud and John Townsend, *Boundaries* (Grand Rapids, MI: Zondervan, 1992), 70.

40   James Strong, *The New Strong's Expanded Exhaustive Concordance of the Bible* (Nashville: Thomas Nelson, 2010), 22-23.

41   Ibid., 98.

42   Henry Cloud and John Townsend, *Boundaries* (Grand Rapids, MI: Zondervan, 1992), 271.

43 James Limburg, *Jonah: A Commentary* (Louisville, KY: Westminster/John Knox Press, 1993), 93.

44 Warren W Wiersbe, *The Wiersbe Bible Commentary: Old Testament* (Colorado Springs, CO: David C Cook, 2007), 1448.

45 Ibid., 876.

46 Warren W Wiersbe, *The Wiersbe Bible Commentary: New Testament* (Colorado Springs, CO: David C Cook, 2007), 853.

47 Pat Layton, *Surrendering the Secret: Healing the Heartbreak of Abortion* (LifeWay Press, 2008), 57.

48 Gary Chapman, *The Other Side of Love*, 36.

CHAPTER 8:   49 Warren Wiersbe, *The Wiersbe Bible Commentary: New Testament*, (Colorado Springs, CO: David C Cook, 2007), 55.

50 *The Holy Bible, Today's New International Version*, (Grand Rapids, MI: Zondervan, 2005), 907.

51 James Strong, *The New Strong's Expanded Exhaustive Concordance of the Bible*, (Nashville, TN: Thomas Nelson, 2010), 74.

52 Verlyn D. Verbrugge, *New International Dictionary of New Testament Theology*, (Grand Rapids, MI: Zondervan, 2000), 204.

53 Paula Rinehardt, *Strong Women Soft Hearts*, (Nashville, TN: Thomas Nelson, 2001), 116.

54 Kelly Minter, *The Fitting Room: Putting on the Character of Christ*, (Colorado Springs, CO: David C Cook, 2011), 88.

55 Ibid., 91-92.

56 Thank you, Christy C, for sharing this example with our group. I'll never forget how you explained what God had revealed for you to do. You are an inspiration!

57 Lewis Smedes, *The Art of Forgiving: When You Need to Forgive and Don't Know How* (New York: Ballantine Books, 1996), 93-94.

58 Ibid., 91.

CHAPTER 9:   59 Thank you, Susan, for your wisdom and insight regarding the "female" version of the holes in our hearts.

CHAPTER 10:   60 Patricia Layton, *Surrendering The Secret* (Nashville, TN: Lifeway Press, 2008), 31.

61 Thank you Flat Irons Community Church for teaching me the "me too" attitude.

CHAPTER 11:   62 Beth Moore, So Long Insecurity: You've been a bad friend to us (Carol Stream, IL: Tyndale House Publishers, 2010), 279-295.

CHAPTER 12:   63 Stephen Arterburn and Jason Martinkus, *Worthy of Her Trust*, (Colorado Springs, CO: WaterBrook Press, 2014), 35.

64 Kelly Minter, *No Other Gods: Confronting Our Modern Day Idols* (Colorado Springs, CO: David C Cook, 2008), 143.

65 Warren Wiersbe, *The Wiersbe Bible Commentary: Old Testament* (Colorado Springs, CO: David C Cooke, 2007), 83.

66 Kelly Minter, *No Other Gods* (Colorado Springs, CO: David C Cook, 2008), 171-172.

67 Derek Kidner, *Proverbs: An Introduction and Commentary* (Downers Grove, IL: Inter-Varsity Press, 1964), 63.

68 Kelly Minter, *Nehemiah* (Nashville, TN: LifeWay Press, 2012), 119.

69 Thank you Chrissie, for giving me this word-picture of God looking me in the eye and being present in the details. I know I miss a lot of God-winks, but when I do see them, it's simply amazing!

70 Jennie Allen, *Anything* (Nashville, TN: Thomas Nelson, 2011), 9.

CHAPTER 13:   71 William M Struthers, *Wired for Intimacy*. (Downers Grove, IL: Intervarsity Press, 2009), 43.

72 Invia Betjoseph, personal communication, October 11, 2014.

73 Patrick Carnes, *Don't Call It Love* (NY: Bantam Books, 1991), 270.

CHAPTER 14:   74 Henry Cloud and John Townsend, *Boundaries* (Grand Rapids, MI: Zondervan, 1992), 62.

CHAPTER 15:   75 Warren W Wiersbe. *The Wiersbe Bible Commentary: The New Testament* (Colorado Springs, CO: David C Cook, 2007), 852.

76 James Strong. *The New Strong's Exhaustive Concordance of the Bible* (Nashville, TN: Thomas Nelson, 2010), 103.

77 Definition of good in English. (n.d.). Retrieved October 8, 2014, from http://www.oxforddictionaries.com/definition/english/good

APPENDIX A: 78 Thank you, Tracy C, for helping me put into words what it looks like to give feedback.

APPENDIX D: 79 Steven Arterburn and Jason Martinkus, *Worthy of Her Trust* (Colorado Springs, CO: Waterbrook Press, 2014), 103.

80 Ibid., 175.

81 Ibid., 173.

ABOUT THE AUTHOR

Shelley Martinkus lives in Denver, Colorado with her husband Jason and their three sons – Truman, Harrison and Norman. Almost twelve years ago, Shelley's life changed forever when she discovered she was married to a sex addict. Her recovery, Shelley admits, has been a slow one. God has been very patient with her. And it's been through this process that God has shown Shelley that He works everything in this life for our good. Shelley enjoys reading books, playing outside with her boys, cuddling and conversing with Jason and running. Shelley has two degrees that were very difficult to obtain (hence the reason it's mentioned) and that have nothing to do with this book (hence the reason there is not need to say what the degrees are in). Shelley would love to connect with you at rlforwomen.com.

CHECK OUT OUR BLOG AND KITCHEN CONVOS AT

www.rlforwomen.com

CPSIA information can be obtained
at www.ICGtesting.com
Printed in the USA
LVOW05s1308081116
512128LV00018B/388/P

9 780982 6382